# THE NEW PAGANS

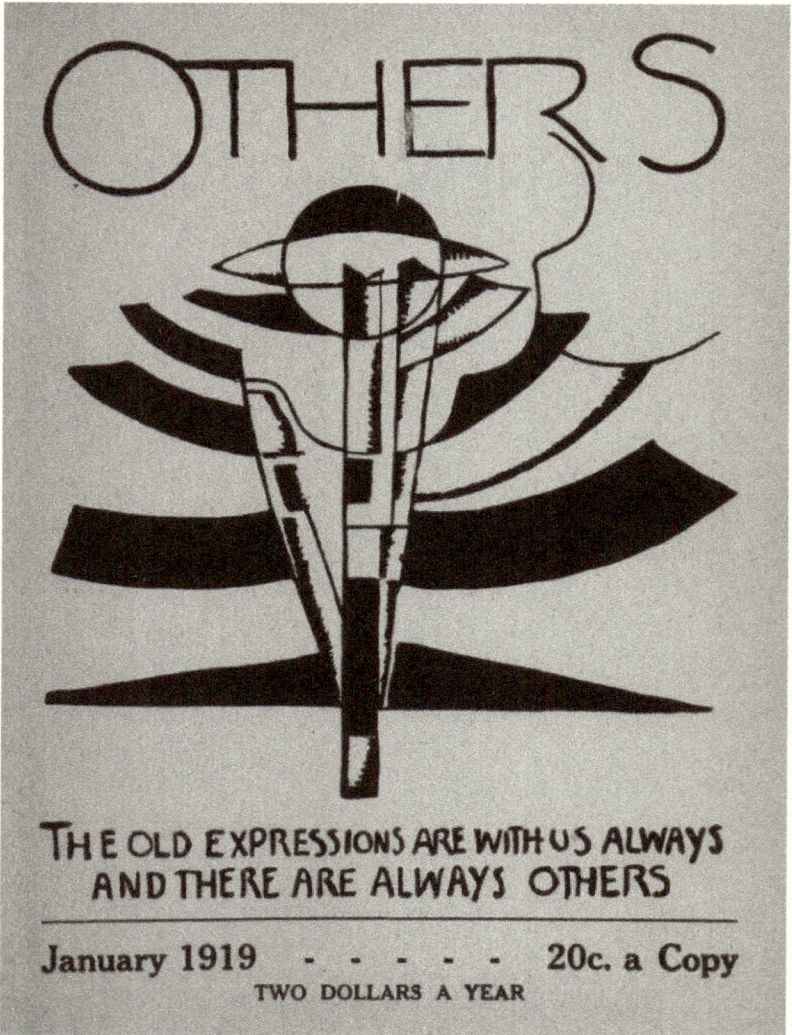

*Margaret Zorach's cover illustration for* Others, *January 1919.*

# THE NEW PAGANS

an anthology of American free verse,
1895-1922

edited by
## PETER NELSON-KING

2018
Redmond, WA

Set in Sylfaen
Titles in Century Gothic

NOTE:
*Every effort has been taken to preserve the formatting and visual effect of the poems reprinted here as they were originally published, but some poems were built for unusual page formats, had apparent spelling inconsistencies or printing errors, or were sourced from volumes that contained typographical ambiguities.  In each instance the editor has taken slight liberties in revising the content and form of the poems to better meld with the formatting limitations of this book.  The majority of spelling and formatting differences between the works of the different poets are due to faithful reproduction of their poems as their appeared in their respective sources.  The editor accepts that some readers may reasonably disagree with his editing decisions.*

# TABLE OF CONTENTS

### A NOTE ON THE "PINS":

The poet Witter Bynner, writing under the pen name Emmanuel Morgan, published a chapbook in 1920 entitled *Pins for Wings*. These "pins" were aphoristic caricatures of his fellow writers and artists, and whenever a poet has been featured here that was the subject of a pin, their applicable pin is included in their section heading

# THE BIRTH OF AMERICAN FREE VERSE

Poetry is a fugitive art – plagued with low sales and misunderstanding, the medium sees many practitioners create fine works which sadly drift and fade in the mist of publishing. A single poem cannot be a product in the way of a novel or even story, and so it is forced into bulk packaging or the more obscure pages of magazines. It is no surprise, then, that the history of poetry has taken a great deal of work to flesh out, as much of the finest verse has fallen into the cracks of memory, requiring great effort to uncover and even more to understand. In American English classes, poetry undergoes a startling bloom around 1920, with the debuts of Frost, Cummings, Williams and many other names that formed the "first" generation of modern American poetry. That bloom, however, is often taught without any date attached to it, as the verse of these writers has survived long after the communities that fostered it. It is also presented without precedent, and understandably so, as the 19th century offered little warning – if more than half a dozen names from that era were even mentioned. There's Poe, Longfellow and Dickinson, and nobody, aside from the singular voice of Walt Whitman, the first writer of what we could call free verse in this country.

Influenced by the Transcendentalists, who occasionally wrote poetry themselves, Whitman's poems could be better called sermons, with their rambling, overflowing lines that espouse a worldly, big-hearted philosophy of life and American identity, and their place in literary history is deservedly secure. That being said, his character and charisma may have been influential to some, but one would be hard pressed to find a poet in the succeeding years who attempted to copy his technique. Some people are simply too famous to ape, and this state of affairs, with all of America's poetry remaining in traditional forms, would continue until the 1910's, with the momentary appearance of Stephen Crane's verse, which will be explored later.

Many theories could be posited for the rise of "little magazines" in the 1910's. By that time literacy in highly populated areas had reached a sufficient level to meet an increased volume in publishing, a volume assured by the proliferation of web offset printing and improved typesetting and paper technology. America was a proud nation coming into the 20th century, and the scientific marvels of automobiles and airplanes, cinema and sound recording allowed for people, messages and imagery to move faster than ever before. Urbanization, and the (somewhat manufactured) reputation of cities like New York and Chicago as venues for success and reinvention created enormous hubs of cultural creation and celebration. When enough people, money and time get together, wonderful things can occur – and so they did. In Chicago, Harriet Monroe, a woman who considered being a poetic figure a life goal, founded *Poetry* in 1912, a publication which to this day continues to be the leading forum for magazine verse. Monroe was a wise, tasteful judge of her fellow writers, and her magazine offered space for conservative authors as well as young ones with unusual ideas. Most of those ideas were born not in America, but in an Avant-Garde fellowship in London.

*The Egoist, The Poetry Bookshop* and other publishing venues were spotlighting the work of the Imagists – a loosely defined collective effort by British authors Richard Aldington, T.S. Eliot and Hilda Doolittle, alongside American expatriates John Gould Fletcher, Ezra Pound and Amy Lowell, and others, to bring poetry into the modern era. In essence, Imagism was a reaction against Romantic poetry norms of strict metrical and rhyming structures, lofty imagery verging on overblown, and wishy-washy emotions. Chief among their influences was ancient poetic traditions from China, Japan and Greece, all of which had been reintroduced to the reading public by a series of acclaimed translations over the past two decades. Epitaphs, haiku and tanka were seen as models of compactness, clarity, and evocation, able to capture sadness and ecstasy, darkness and light, with only a few pen strokes. After a couple years of publication in London, Imagism was brought to New York, with *Des Imagistes*, the first anthology of Imagist verse on its own, seeing publication in 1914. American book publishers took note, encouraged by Lowell's previous establishment in the U.S., and Houghton Mifflin published free verse books by Fletcher, as well as the eccentric Walter Arensberg. Lowell published her new work with Harcourt Brace, her publisher of three years prior.

In New York, another scene was brewing. 1913 saw the famous International Exhibition of Modern Art, nicknamed the Armory Show, and its first stop was New York on Lexington Ave. The show introduced Americans to the latest trends in painting, sculpture and photography from Europe, including fledgling Cubism and Dadaism. Around the same time Alfred Stieglitz, a photographer and artistic impresario, had established the 291 Gallery on 5th Ave, which hosted the work of leading American photographers as well as many of the same European artists featured in the Armory show. His circle of collaborators grew to include writers, not in the least the pseudo-Dadaist work of his frequent model Katharine N. Rhoades, but most importantly Alfred Kreymborg, who had the privilege of reading a manuscript of *Des Imagistes* by way of his friend Ezra Pound. Kreymborg was a man of seemingly infinite energies and near infinite friendships, and in 1913 he founded *The Glebe*, a very short-lived periodical that devoted entire issues to single writers' work. From that fledgling effort he founded *Others* in 1915, arguably, aside from *Poetry*, the most important little magazine of the time dedicated wholly to verse. In 1916 Kreymborg would publish the first book of his own verse, *Mushrooms*, which was quickly recognized for Kreymborg's humorous, unusual verse-style.

*Others*'s contributors, and associate editor slate, included William Carlos Williams, Wallace Stevens and Marianne Moore, as well T.S. Eliot and fellow British authors Mina Loy, and John Rodker, with many others in tow to make for a reading experience unlike any other. It's influence was quickly reflected in the premiere of *The Pagan* in 1916, a more obscure publication that saw the first print of dozens of modernist poets, most of whom disappeared into the ether. An important cross-format little magazine with national reach, Margaret Anderson's *The Little Review*, mixed poetry with stories, editorial articles, and a vibrant letters section that has become almost as famous and studied as its body content. The *Review* was the debut venue for "Baroness Elsa",

3

the first Dadaist poet to publish in the U.S., and her multi-page, baffling word paintings caused an uproar among the *Review*'s readership.

Thousands of miles away, Chicago was undergoing a cultural renaissance. The 1910's and '20's were a time of immense artistic activity and growth in the Midwestern metropolis, and *Poetry* was only a small part of it. A great number of brilliant painters, composers, writers and photographers comingled at the time, with its writing scene producing figures who would go on to national prominence. This was the world of Maxwell Bodenheim, who would later be known as king of the Greenwich Village Bohemians, and Ben Hecht, who would become one of Hollywood's greatest screenwriters. Both of them published free verse of creativity and distinction. At the beginning of the '20's the publishers Pascal Covici, who would eventually serve as chief editor of Viking Press, and Monroe Wheeler, a major member of the American expatriate community in between the wars, would issue their first books, including the freshman efforts of Glenway Wescott and Mark Turbyfill. A curious chapbook firm named Musterbookhouse would exist just long enough to issue a collection of George Grosz's lithographs, as well as *The Magpie's Shadow*, a cycle of one-line poems by the young Yvor Winters. And of course, Chicago was the home of Carl Sandburg, whose *Chicago Poems* from 1916 was immediately recognized as one of the boldest and most endearing books in American verse.

The swift attention that free verse had been awarded nationwide was a remarkable feat, so much so that spoofs soon appeared. In 1916 the New York poets Witter Bynner and Arthur Davison Ficke published *Spectra* under the names of Emmanuel Morgan and Anne Knish, purportedly a collection of "Spectrist" verse that lampooned Imagism. A third "Spectrist", Elijah Hay, was the pseudonym of Marjorie Allen Seiffert, whose Spectrist verse wouldn't see print until 1919. Critics were so overwhelmed by the overnight recognition of Imagism that many of them took Spectrism as a legitimate movement upon *Spectra*'s publication, not catching on until Bynner and Ficke announced the hoax publicly. Alfred A. Knopf, then a new publisher, issued follow-up books from Bynner and Seiffert that would be career high points for both poets, and was part of what established Knopf as one of America's greatest publishers. They were also responsible for reprint Adelaide Crapsey's posthumous collection *Verse*, the first proof that an American could create a new verse format and master it completely.

In 1922 Harcourt Brace, already established as a champion of modernist verse with their support of Amy Lowell (and later Alfred Kreymborg), published two parody books of everybody from Imagists to other rising stars like Robert Frost and Vachel Lindsay. The first, Margaret Widdemer's *A Tree With A Bird In It*, was "a symposium" of contemporary "poets" writing on the common image of a grackle sitting in a pear tree. The second, *Heavens*, was the creation of Louis Untermeyer, one of the greatest poetry anthologists of the first half of the 20th century, and depicted a man touring Heaven and seeing literary developments within, followed by parody poems in the style of various contemporaries with their names encoded with hyphens. It was clear from these efforts that free verse, and American poetry, had come into its own.

1922 is a fair stopping point for this anthology, and not merely because of copyright concerns that I will freely admit. 1923 might be a contender for the most important year in American verse, as it saw the publication of Wallace Stevens's first book *Harmonium*, William Carlos Williams's *Spring and All*, and E.E. Cummings's *Tulips & Chimneys*. Cummings had previously had a few poems published in *Eight Harvard Poets* (alongside Robert Hillyer and John Dos Passos) and *Broom*, the next periodical begun by Kreymborg after *Others* folded. The year after that saw the publication of Marianne Moore's *Observations*, the first authorized book of her poems and still one of the most revered single volumes of American verse. In this sense, 1922 was the last year of American poetry's adolescence, of free experimentation, outside of economic and social constraints. Imagism had its rules, but they were loosely enforced, and no two practitioners were alike. Free verse as a whole was brilliantly diverse, and that diversity allowed Stevens, Williams, Sandburg, Moore and Cummings to become the standard bearers of modern American poetry. America had no poetic tradition before them, and the splash they made was so resounding that, along with traditionalists, America had its first poetic generation, one that allowed free verse to continue in the mainstream much longer than

5

it did in England, where Aldington, Pound and Doolittle were always erudite outliers. Eliot's *The Waste Land* was immediately influential, but those who tried to imitate his style were largely seen as failures (like Aldington, with his book *A Fool i' the Forest*).

In 1922, Robert Alden Sanborn, a Boston native who wrote highly varied free verse in the 1910's and was a great asset to the New York scene, published "A Champion in the Wilderness", an article praising the short-lived little magazine *The Soil*, in that year's October issue of *Broom*. His article spoke of *The Soil* in relation to little magazines like *Others*, saying that the scenes of 1916 were "a magic moment. No one who was touched by the kindling breath will ever forget the joy of it nor cease to regret that a great fiery wind devoured it. It will be worth some day to review that frail but vital page in American literary history."

This book was born out of a similar sentiment, which in itself was born from curiosity, the curiosity of an amateur, recently-inspired lover of American poetry. My background is music and composition, and the first times that I had heard the names of Alfred Kreymborg, Amy Lowell and Mark Turbyfill were through obscure musical works that I admired. As I discovered these authors, through their own books as well as anthologies like the *Others* collections, I realized that there was a whole world of modern poetry that had become totally invisible. This invisibility helped me understand how legends like Cummings and Sandburg could become so established at all, and who encouraged them to write simply by creating fine work around them. Much of my musical career has been dedicated to unearthing great works by unknown composers, and this project has been another expression of that same sentiment. As such, the early work of Sandburg, Cummings, Williams, Stevens, Moore and Pound has been left out of this anthology, partially because their work has received an enormous amount of attention for decades, and mostly to leave more room for unknowns and eccentrics like William Saphier and the Baroness Elsa. In the case of a few writers, like Katharine N. Rhoades, Ruth Suckow and Routledge Curry, I have reprinted the whole of their published verse, as it appears that no one else has bothered. The books that bear the names of many of these writers have been out of print since their first publications, and thus are very rare, frequently demanding

6

high prices from booksellers. It's my hope, by making this work more freely available, and curated to make a comprehensive picture of the atmosphere in which it was created, that more people will seek it out, and maybe someday we'll see modern reprints and critical reappraisals of what should be considered the bedrock of American poetry.

The motto of *Others*, as seen in the cover reproduced for this book's frontispiece, reads *"THE OLD EXPRESSIONS ARE WITH US ALWAYS AND THERE ARE ALWAYS OTHERS"*. This book is dedicated to the Others, past, present and future.

**Peter Nelson-King**
**August 2018**

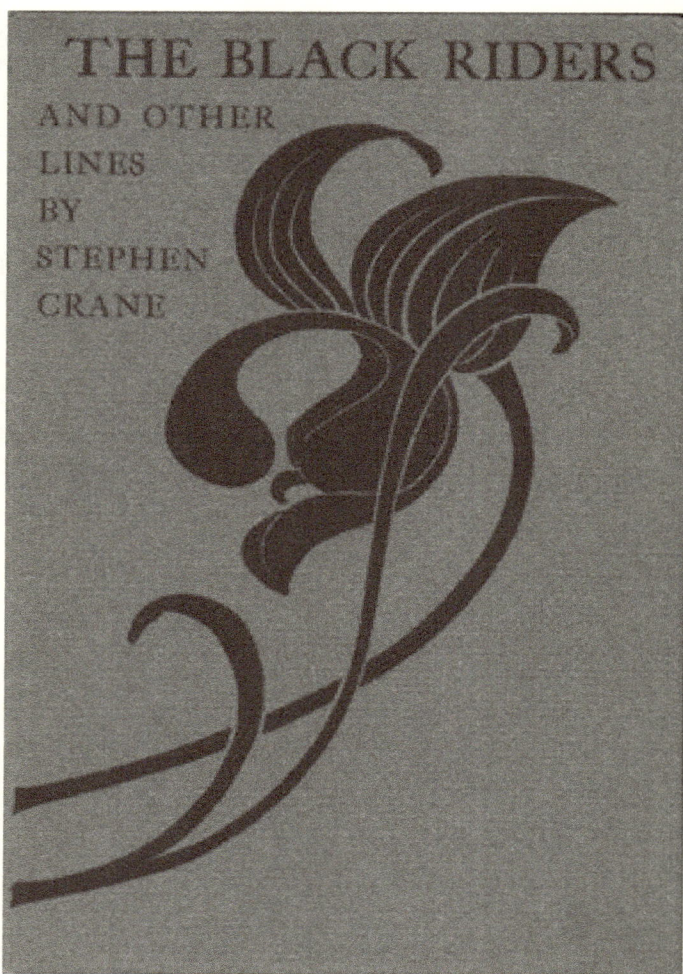

*The cover of Stephen Crane's* The Black Riders, *1895, 1st edition.*

# PRELUDE: VOX CLAMENS IN ALTERUM

## Stephen Crane – Selections from *The Black Riders*

*While some may point to the glorious rambling of Walt Whitman as the first free verse written in America, in the editor's opinion there is only one true predecessor to the early years of free verse – the strange lines of Stephen Crane. Crane had distinguished himself in the early 1890's with* The Red Badge of Courage, *his intensely psychological study of Civil War soldiers, and its success brought him into the company of William Dean Howells, who introduced him to the work of Emily Dickinson. Inspired by Dickinson's effortless wisdom and structural concision, Crane set out to write his own verse – and the result was* The Black Riders and Other Lines. *Comprising 54 scenes and aphorisms, the "lines" are all composed in a sparse, unmetered structure that complements Crane's pessimistic, often apocalyptic world. They were received as well as they could be by an American reading public not used to surreal darkness, and as of present there is nothing in literature quite like them, or nearly as memorable.*

I.

Black riders came from the sea.
There was a clang and clang of spear and
                shield,
and clash and clash of hoof and heel,
wild shouts and the wave of hair
in the rush upon the wind:
thus the ride of sin.

III.

In the desert
I saw a creature, naked, bestial,

who, squatting upon the ground,
held his heart in his hands,
and ate of it.
I said, "Is it good, friend?"
"It is bitter – bitter," he answered;
"But I like it
"because it is bitter,
"and because it is my heart."

IV.

Yes, I have a thousand tongues,
and nine and ninety-nine lie.
Though I strive to use the one,
it will make no melody at my will,
but is dead in my mouth.

IX.

I stood upon a high place,
and saw, below, many devils
running, leaping,
and carousing in sin.
One looked up, grinning,
and said, "Comrade! Brother!"

XIII.

If there is a witness to my little life,
to my tiny throes and struggles,
he sees a fool;
and it is not fine for gods to menace
        fools.

XX.

A learned man came to me once.
He said, "I know the way, - come."

And I was overjoyed at this.
Together we hastened.
Soon, too soon, were we
where my eyes were useless,
and I knew not the ways of my feet.
I clung to the hand of my friend;
but at last he cried, "I am lost."

XXXII.

Two or three angels
came near to the earth.
They saw a fat church.
Little black streams of peple
came and went in continually.
And the angels were puzzled
to know why the people went thus,
and why they stayed so long within.

XXXVII.

On the horizon the peaks assembled;
and as I looked,
the march of the mountains began.
As they marched, they sang,
"Aye!  We come!  We come!"

# DES IMAGISTES

As influential as it is difficult to categorize, the short-lived movement of Imagism is the *de facto* birth of modernist verse in English. First created in England in the early 1910's and then transplanted, the genre, as codified as it ever was, eschewed the traditional meters, overblown sentiments and mushy imagery common to Romantic poetry in favor of concision, clarity and freedom of line, allowing the right words to stand on their own feet.

A collective of poets formed in London, beginning with the tragically short-lived T.E. Hulme and gaining definition with figures such as Richard Aldington, Ford Madox Ford and T.S. Eliot, as well as American expatriates like Ezra Pound and Hilda Doolittle. Their work was influenced by ancient, foreign forms, such as Japanese haiku and tanka and Greek aphorisms, and trafficked in imagery both natural and exotic, psychological and earthbound. The connection with American letters brought their work to the U.S. with a series of seminal anthologies and appearances in "little" magazines, then a newly burgeoning venue for modernist literature. Quickly thereafter, American poets in their home country took up the cause, such as with the epic, iconoclastic work of Amy Lowell, the mysterious epigrams of Skipwith Cannéll, and many others. The genre would supply the formal basis for the debuts of major figures like Wallace Stevens and William Carlos Williams, and its impact on the American scene cemented its authors as standard-bearers for their home country's newly-made poetic tradition, in contrast to its relegation as a passing fad in England. As Imagism was never a formalized movement, its practitioners moved on to form more personal voices, but the shockwaves it created in American art will never be forgotten.

## Amy Lowell – Selections from *Men, Women and Ghosts*

Pin:
A rhinestone chip
On a blood-red shoulder

*Chief among American Imagists was the great Amy Lowell (1874-1926), whose difficult formative years helped produce an iconoclast of enormous value to American letters. An unusual presence with her lack of a college education, her love of smoking cigars in public, and noticeably rotund figure, she was once unkindly called the "hippopoetess" by the poet Witter Bynner. Lowell made a meal of her position as a square peg and developed a highly personal yet worldly poetic voice, one that won her the admiration of her colleagues and eventually the Pulitzer Prize, though only a year after her untimely death at the age of 51. Initially mastering traditional forms, Lowell invented a prose-poetry style fellow Imagist John Gould Fletcher dubbed "polyphonic prose". Her many long narrative poems, which blur the line between verse and short story, make her most representative work difficult to anthologize. The three pieces here all come from her 1917 book* Men, Women and Ghosts, *and feature many attributes that are hallmarks of her work – a mixture of wonder and sadness, focusing on people trapped in emotional isolation, and onomatopoeic tone-painting that looks forward to the work of E. E. Cummings.*

### THE DINNER-PARTY

I. FISH

"So…" they said,
With their wine-glasses delicately poised,
Mocking at the thing they cannot understand.
"So…" they said again,
Amused and insolent.
The silver on the table glittered,

**14**

And the red wine in the glasses
Seemed the blood I had wasted
In a foolish cause.

II. GAME

The gentleman with the grey-and-black whiskers
Sneered languidly over his quail.
Then my heart flew up and labored,
And I burst from my own holding
And hurled myself forward.
With straight blows I beat upon him,
Furiously, with red-hot anger, I thrust against him.
But my weapon slithered over his polished surface,
And I recoiled upon myself,
Panting.

III. DRAWING-ROOM

In a dress all softness and half-tones,
Indolent and half-reclined,
She lay upon a couch,
With the firelilght reflected in her jewels.
But her eyes had no reflection,
They swam in a grey smoke,
The smoke of smouldering ashes,
The smoke of her cindered heart.

IV. COFFEE

They sat in a circle with their coffee-cups.
One dropped in a lump of sugar,
One stirred with a spoon.
I saw them as a circle of ghosts
Sipping blackness out of beautiful china,
And mildly protesting against my coarseness
In being alive.

## V. TALK

They took dead men's souls
And pinned them on their breasts for ornament;
Their cuff-links and tiaras
Were gems dug from a grave;
They were ghouls battening on exhumed thoughts;
And I took a green liqueur from a servant
So that he might come near me
And give me the comfort of a living thing.

## VI. ELEVEN O'CLOCK

The front door was hard and heavy,
It shut behind me on the house of ghosts.
I flattened my feet on the pavement
To feel it solid under me;
I ran my hand along the railings
And shook them,
And pressed their pointed bars
Into my palms.
The hurt of it reassured me,
And I did it again and again
Until they were bruised.
When I woke in the night
I laughed to find them aching,
For only living flesh can suffer.

## THE PAPER WINDMILL

The little boy pressed his face against the window-pane and looked out at the bright sunshiny morning. The cobble-stones of the square glistened like mica. In the trees, a breeze danced and pranced, and shook drops of sunlight like falling golden coins into the brown water of the canal. Down stream slowly drifted a long string of galliots piled with crimson cheeses. The little boy thought they looked as if they were roc's eggs, blocks of big ruby eggs. He

16

said, "Oh!" with delight, and pressed against the window with all his might.

The golden cock on top of the *Stadhuis* gleamed. His beak was open like a pair of scissors and a narrow piece of blue sky was wedged in it. "Cock-a-doodle'do," cried the little boy. "Can't you hear me through the window, Gold Cocky? Cock-a-doodle-do! You should crow when you see the eggs of your cousin, the great roc." But the golden cock stood stock still, with his fine tail blowing in the wind. He could not understand the little boy, for he said "*Cocorico*" when he said anything. But he was hung in the air to swing, not to sing. His eyes glittered to the bright West wind, and the crimson cheeses drifted away down the canal.

It was very dull there in the big room. Outside in the square, the wind was playing tag with some fallen leaves. A man passed, with a dogcart beside him full of smart, new milkcans. They rattled out a gay tune: "Tiddity-tum-ti-ti. Have some milk for your tea. Cream for your coffee to drink to-night, thick, and smooth, and sweet, and white," and the man's sabots beat an accompaniment: "Plop! Trop! Milk for your tea. Plop! Trop! Drink it to-night." It was very pleasant out there, but it was lonely here in the big room. The little boy gulped at a tear.

It was queer how dull all his toys were. They were so still. Nothing was still in the square. If he took his eyes away a moment it had changed. The milkman had disappeared round the corner, there was only an old woman with a basket of green stuff on her head, picking her way over the shiny stones. But the wind pulled the leaves in the basket this way and that, and displayed them to beautiful advantage. The sun patted them condescendingly on their flat surfaces, and they seemed sprinkled with silver. The little boy sighed as he looked at his disordered toys on the floor. They were motionless, and their colours were dull. The dark wainscoting absorbed the sun. There was none left for toys.

The square was quite empty now. Only the wind ran round and round it, spinning. Away over in the corner where a street

17

opened into the square, the wind had stopped. Stopped running, that is, for it never stopped spinning. It whirred, and whirled, and gyrated, and turned. It burned like a great coloured sun. It hummed, and bussed, and sparked, and darted. There were flashes of blue, and long smearing lines of saffron, and quick jabs of green. And over it all was a sheen like a myriad cut diamonds. Round and round it went, the huge wind-wheel, and the little boy's head reeled with watching it. The whole square was filled with its rays, blazing and leaping round after one another, faster and faster. The little boy could not speak, he could only gaze, staring in amaze.

The wind-wheel was coming down the square. Nearer and nearer it came, a great disk of spinning flame. It was opposite the window now, and the little boy could see it plainly, but it was something more than the wind which he saw. A man was carrying a huge fan-shaped frame on his shoulder, and stuck in it were many little painted paper windmills, each one scurrying round in the breeze. They were bright and beautiful, and the sight was one to please anybody, and how much more a little boy who had only stupid, motionless toys to enjoy.

The little boy clapped his hands, and his eyes danced and whizzed, for the circling windmills made him dizzy. Closer and closer came the windmill man, and held up his big fan to the little boy in the window of the Ambassador's house. Only a pane of glass between the boy and the windmills. They slid round before his eyes in rapidly revolving splendor. There were wheels and wheels of colours – big, little, thick, thin – all one clear, perfect spin. The windmill vendor dipped and raised them again, and the little boy's face was glued to the windowpane. Oh! What a glorious, wonderful plaything! Rings and rings of windy colour always moving! How had any one ever preferred those other toys which never stirred. "Nursie, come quickly. Look! I want a windmill. See! It is never still. You will buy me one, won't you? I want the silver one, with the big ring of blue."

So a servant was sent to buy that one: silver, ringed with blue, and smartly it twirled about in the servant's hands as he stood a moment to pay the vendor. Then he entered the house, and in another minute he was standing in the nursery door, with some crumpled paper on the end of a stick which he held out to the little boy. "But I wanted a windmill which went round," cried the little boy. "That is the one you asked fr, Master Charles," Nursie was a bit impatient, she had mending to do. "See, it is silver, and here is the blue." "But it is only a blue streak," sobbed the little boy. "I wanted a blue ring, and this silver doesn't sparkle." "Well, Master Charles, that is what you wanted, now run away and play with it, for I am very busy."

The little boy hid his tears against the friendly window-pane. On the floor lay the motionless, crumpled bit of paper on the end of its stick. But far away across the square was the windmill vendor, with his big wheel of whirring splendor. It spun round in a blaze like a whirling rainbow, and the sun gleamed upon it, and the wind whipped it until it seemed a maze of spattering diamonds. "*Cocorico!*" crowed the golden cock on the top of the *Stadhuis*. "That is something worth crowing for." But the little boy did not hear him, he was sobbing over the crumpled bit of paper on the floor.

## STRAVINSKY'S THREE PIECES, "GROTESQUES", FOR STRING QUARTET

FIRST MOVEMENT

Thin-voiced, nasal pipes
Drawing sound out and out
Until it is a screeching thread,
Sharp and cutting, sharp and cutting,
It hurts.
Whee-e-e!
Bump! Bump! Tong-ti-bump!
There are drums here,
Banging.

And wooden shoes beating the round, grey stones
Of the market-place.
Whee-e-e!
Sabots slapping the worn, old stones,
And a shaking and cracking of dancing bones;
Clumsy and hard they are,
And uneven,
Losing half a beat
Because the stones are slippery.
Bomp-e-ty-tong! Whee-e-e! Tong!
The thin Spring leaves
Shake to the banging of shoes.
Shoes beat, slap,
Shuffle, rap,
And the nasal pipes squeal with their pigs' voices,
Little pigs' voices
Weaving among the dancers,
A fine white thread
Linking up the dancers.
Bang! Bump! Tong!
Petticoats,
Stockings,
Sabots,
Delirium flapping its thigh-bones;
Red, blue, yellow,
Drunkenness steaming in colours;
Red, yellow, blue,
Colours and flesh weaving together,
In and out, with the dance, coarse stuffs and hot
flesh weaving together.
Pigs' cries white and tenuous,
White and painful,
White and –
Bump!
Tong!

SECOND MOVEMENT

Pale violin music whiffs across the moon,
A pale smoke of violin music blown over the moon,
Cherry petals fall and flutter,
And the white Pierrot,
Wreathed in the smoke of the violins,
Splashed with cherry petals falling, falling,
Claws a grave for himself in the fresh earth
With his finger-nails.

THIRD MOVEMENT

An organ growls in the heavy roof-groins of a
church,
It wheezes and coughs.
The nave is blue with incense,
Writhing, twisting,
Snaking over the heads of the chanting priests.
        *Requiem aternam dona ei, Domine;*
The priests whine their bastard Latin
And the censers swing and click.
The priests walk endlessly
Round and round,
Droning their Latin
Off the key.
The organ crashes out in a flaring chord,
And the priests hitch their chant up half a tone.
        *Dies illa, dies iræ,*
        *Calamitatis et miseriæ,*
        *Dies magna et amara valde.*
A wind rattles the leaded windows.
The little pear-shaped candle flames leap and
flutter,
        *Dies illa, dies iræ;*
The swaying smoke drifts over the altar,
        *Calamitatis et miseriæ;*
The shuffling priests sprinkle holy water,

*Dies magna et amara valde;*
And there is a stark stillness in the midst of them
Stretched upon a bier.
His ears are stone to the organ,
His eyes are flint to the candles,
His body is ice to the water.
Chant, priests,
Whine, shuffle, genuflect,
He will always be as rigid as he is now
Until he crumbles away in a dust heap.

*Lacrymosa dies illa,*
*Qua resurget ex favilla*
*Judicandus homo reus.*

Above the grey pillars the roof is in darkness.

## Skipwith Cannéll – "Nocturnes" and others

*More than any other American Imagist, Skipwith Cannéll (1887-1957) typified many of the traits of early Imagism: brevity and concreteness, with a fixation on antique themes and exoticism. As a close friend of William Carlos Williams and Ezra Pound, Cannéll's poems were included in the first Imagist anthology,* Des Imagistes, *as well as in Harriet Monroe's* The New Poetry, *arguably the most important guidebook to American poetry from the first part of the 20th century. Closely associated with* Others, *a seminal magazine for modernist poetry of the 1910's and 20's, Cannéll was nevertheless an elusive figure and to this day little of his work survives, none of it formally collected. His set "Nocturnes" was especially praised and has been anthologized many times, and the poems' austerity and compactness are models for the first new forms in English poetry of the century.*

### NOCTURNES

I.

Thy feet,
That are like little, silver birds,
Thou hast set upon pleasant ways;
Therefore I will follow thee,
Thou Dove of the Golden Eyes,
Upon any path will I follow thee,
For the light of thy beauty
Shines before me like a torch.

II.

Thy feet are white
Upon the foam of the sea;
Hold me fast, thouh bright Swan,
Lest I stumble,
And into deep waters.

III.

Long have I been
But the Singer beneath thy Casement,
And now I am weary.
I am sick with longing,
O my Belovéd;
Therefore bear me with thee
Swiftly
Upon our road.

IV.

With the net of thy hair
Thou has fished in the sea,
And a strange fish
Has thou caught in thy net;
For thy hair,
Beloved,
Holdeth my heart
Within its web of gold.

V.

I am weary with love, and thy lips
Are night-born poppies.
Give me therefore thy lips
That I may know sleep.

VI.

I am weary with longing,
I am faint with love;
For upon my head has the moonlight
Fallen
As a sword.

# THE RED BRIDGE

The arches of the red bridge
Are stronger than ever;
The arches of the scarlet bridge
Are of rough, bleak stone.

(Why should such massive arches be the span
        From cloud to tenuous cloud?)

Let us not seek omens in the guts
Of newly slain fowls;
Leaving such play to the children,
Let us pluck wild swans
        From under the moon;
Or, challenging strong, terrible me,
        Let us slay them and seek truth
                In their smoking entrails.

Let us fling runners
        Across the red bridge,
Deep-lunged runners who will return to us
With tidings of the far countries
And the strange seas!

There be many terrible men
Going out upon the bridge,
Through the little door
        That is by the steps from the river.


# THE COMING OF NIGHT
        (In the city)

The sun is near set
And the tall buildings
Become teeth
Tearing bloodily at the sky's throat;

The blank wall by my window
Becomes night sky over the marshes
When there is no moon, and no wind,
And little fishes splash in the pools.

I had lit my candle to make a song for you,
But I have forgotten it for I am very tired;
And the candle...a yellow moth...
Flutters, flutters,
Deep in my brain.
My song was about, 'a foreign lady
Who was beautiful and sad,
Who was forsaken, and who died
A thousand years ago.'
But the cracked cup at my elbow,
With dregs of tea in it,
Fixes my tired thought more surely
Than the song I made for you and forgot...
That I might give you *this*.

I am tired.

I am so tired
That my soul is a great plain
Made desolate,
And the beating of a million hearts
Is but the whisper of night winds
Blowing across it.

## John Gould Fletcher – "Orange Symphony"

Pin:
two halves of a typewriter
still moving

*The first Southern poet to win the Pulitzer Prize, John Gould Fletcher (1886-1950) was one of the most famous and revered of card-carrying Imagists. While some poets who bore the Imagist label resented the term, Fletcher championed it, even long after the movement had dissipated. Fellow Imagists Amy Lowell and Ezra Pound thought him a master of the new form, praising his long, imaginative poems that captured light and sensation like a fine painter. The editor believes him to be a spiritual successor to the painter James McNeill Whistler, whose Impressionist canvases with titles like "Nocturne in Black and Gold" and "Symphony in White" are perfect complements to Fletcher's "Symphonies" from his first books. "Orange Symphony" comes from his second book,* Goblins and Pagodas*, which remains one of the finest collections of Imagist verse.*

I.

Now that all the world is filled
With armies clamouring;
Now that men no longer live and die, one by one,
But in vague indeterminate multitudes:

Now that the trees are coppery towers,
Now that the clouds loom southward,
Now that the glossy creeper
Spatters the walls like spilt wine:

I will go out alone,
To catch strong joy of solitude
Where the treelines, in gold and scarlet,
Swing strong grape-cables up the smouldering face
    of the hill.

II.

Guns crashing,
Thudding,
Ululating,
Tumultuous.
Guns yelping over the cracked earth,
Where dry bugles blare.

Here in this hollow
It is very quiet,
Only the wind's hissing laughter
In the space of tombs.

One by one these gaunt scarred faces
Lift up blurred wrinkled inscriptions
Silently beseeching me to stop and ponder.
What does it matter if I do not stop to read them?
No one at all has gone this way that I have chosen
before.

A leaf drops slowly in silence;
It is a long time twisting and hovering on its way to
    the earth.

Guns booming,
Bellowing,
Crashing,
Desperate.
Insistent outcry of savage guns,
Rocking the gloomy hollow.
I will run out like the wind,
Snarling, with savage laughter;
Like the wind that tosses the grey-black clouds,
Against the shot-racked barrier of flaming trees.

I will race between the grey guns,

And the clouds, like shrapnel exploding,
Flinging their hail through the tumult,
Bursting, will melt in cold spray.

I am the wanderer of the world;
No one can hold me.
Not the cannon assembled for battle,
Nor the gloomy graves of the hollow,
Nor the house where I long time slumbered,
Nor the hilltop where roads are straggling.
My feet must march to the wind.

Like a leaf dropping slowly,
An orange butterfly turning and twisting,
I touch with moist passionate palms the leaden
        inscriptions
Of my past.  Then I turn to depart.

III.

The trees dance about the inn;
The wind thrusts them into flamelets.
Now my thoughts gipsying,
Go forth to strange walls and new fires.

Mouths stained with brown-red berries,
Bronzed cheeks sunken, unshave,
Ragged attire;
We swing our guitars at the hip
As we tramp heedless, uncaring.
In the inn the fire crackles:
On the hearth the wind is simmering.
Lift up the brown beaker one instant,
Drink deeply – fling out the last coin – let us go.
On the plains there is drooping harvest,
But no harvest can for long time hold us,
We have seen the winds, baffled,
Racing up the orange-flecked trench of the hills.

IV.

On the hill summit
Where the gusty wind all night long has assailed me,
Now I see stars vanishing
Before the long cold clutching fingers of dawn.

Stars scintillant, fire-hued, metallic,
Topaz fruit of the deep-blue garden:
Southward you go, my constellations,
And leave me with the white day, alone.

Over the hilltop
Swish with a scurry of wings
Millions of pale brown birds,
Songless, pulsing southward.

Birds who have filled the trees,
And who fled long ago at my passing,
Now you clatter in heedless tumult,
Fanning with your hot wings my face.

Carry this word to the southward;
Say that I have forgotten them that wait for me,
All the loves and the hates need expect me no longer,
In the autumn at last I am alone.

Suddenly
The wind crashes through the three-tops,
Stripping away their orange-tiled domes;
Stark blue skeletons, forbidding
Gesticulate in my face.
You whom I planted and lavished
With all the wealth and beauty I had to bestow
Hurry away, vain harvest,
The winds' scythes can reap you,
Where you lie on the earth, and to death's barns you

can go.

Beyond the hilltop
I have seen only the sky.
The wind, naked, prodding up black-furred clouds,
Cossacks of winter.

Cry, wind,
Shriek to the shivering southland,
That I am going into winter,
That I do not hope to return.

Farewell, crowded stars,
Farewell, birds, winds, clouds and treetops,
I, weary of you all, seek my destined joy in the north-
    land,
Amid blue ice and the rose-purple night of the pole.

V.

Beyond the land there lies the sea;
And on the sea with wings unfurled,
Bloodily huge the sunset rests,
Feathers flickering and claws curled,
Watching to seize the ruined world.

Rolling in a torrent,
Brown leaves, my achievements,
Rise up from dark-wooded valleys
And scatter themselves on the sea;
Brown birds, my wild dreams,
Mingle their bodies together,
Shrieking and clamouring as they pass,
Black charred silhouettes
Against the west, curtained in orange flame.
Now the wind starts up
And strikes the seething water:
Hissing in uncoiled fury

Each foam-curled wave darts forward
To clash and batter
The smouldering iron-rust cliff,
Where the end of my road is lost.

Rise up, black clouds;
Pounce upon the sunset:
Tear it with your jagged teeth.
Fling yourselves, seething winds, in circles
Upon the blue-black water,
Swirl, leaves, and dance
Amid the chaos of breakers,
Flicker, birds, an instant
Against the tawny tiger throat of the sun
Which is snarling in the west.
Beat down, O great winds, westward,
Loose reins and gallop to seaward,
Rush me, too, to that ocean,
In which I have found my goal.

Lash me, lap me, rugged waves of blue-black water,
Dash me, clutch me and do not let me rest one instant;
All through the purple-blue night rock and soothe me,
Till I awaken dreamingly at the faint rose breast of the
dawn.

## Frances Gregg – Selections from *Poetry* and *Others*

*Frances Gregg (1885-1941) is one of the unluckier voices to emerge in the early free verse days. A born Midwesterner and suffragette, she became an intense object of love and fascination for the English novelist John Cowper Powys, whom she met in Philadelphia. He convinced her to marry his close friend Louis Wilkinson, but his feelings for her strained and eventually ruined their relationship, and he fell into a serious depression – followed by the breakup of Frances's marriage. Her friendship with the brightest stars of literary modernism in England, including Yeats, Pound, and Hilda Doolittle, didn't keep her from having a difficult life with a child in tow, and in 1941 she was killed during an air raid on London. More than 50 years later her memoir,* The Mystic Leeway, *was published; the rest of her writing remains uncollected. Gregg was perhaps the writer most strongly influenced by Hilda Doolittle, as her verse shares similar fascinations with ancient austerity, soft-edged fragments of imagery, and an air of resignation. As her memoir was largely pitched on its reminiscences of other writers, a full critical appraisal of her verse may never come, but the editor wishes to reprint as much as taste will allow to illustrate her contribution as one of America's first female modernist poets.*

### PERCHÉ

I am the possessor and the possessed.
I am of the unborn.
My kind have not yet come upon the earth.
*Or – are they gone?*
Am I then left, a memory of the dead?
Am I dream-wraith, a ghost of beauty fled?
I who possess and am possessed,
*Am I born and dead?*

Strange madnesses beset me.
Passing pageant-wise across my web of thought.
The red circlet of Narcissus gems my blood, -

And I brook on a golden reed.
Who doth possess me – I possess.
*Yea, I am dead!*

> *In the pale light from the grave*
> > *The Sisters weave:*
> > *Crimson – and green and golden thread*
> > *Upon Time's robe.*

## TO H. D.

You were all loveliness to me –
Sea-mist, the spring,
The blossoming of trees,
The wind,
Giver-of-Dreams.
Then –
A wistful silence guarded you about,
As in the spring
Iris and anemone are guarded.
And like a flame
Your beauty burned and wrought me
Into a bell,
Whose single note
Was echo of your silence.
Now –
You sing.
And I, muted,
Yet vibrate throughout,
Stirred by your hymn's immemorial burden;
"Spare us from loveliness!"

## LES OMBRES DE LA MER

I grieve my dream:
My dream that was like a golden lacquered bowl,

My dream that was coloured like a Chinese print.
A wave of the sea has been here:
Muffled bells and red
Sea-stained gold:
Green flames under the foam,
The blue shadows darting like fishes.
Tread softly:
Do not cleave the air with Thy presence,
I guard my dead from the waters.


### HERMAPHRODITUS

As if the soul of all this pulsing world had taken form
                                                    in thee,-
That thy face should be the flow of waters:
Thy voice the surge of many restless waters:
Thine eyes, envisioning night and all the depths on
            depths of stars therein,
Should be the secret depths of waters:
Thy body's length the grace and suppleness
Of flowers upstanding from the earth.

And I have watched the mystic worry of thy face,
Upturned against the stars and wind,
Grow strange and sad.
Have felt the music that my hands awoke,
Have felt thee start and quiver
And marveled how all parts of thee attuned.


### QUEST

Mist
Grey
Tremulous
And a mighty current beat:
Then sound ceased

35

And light was all,
Restless, tumultuous,
Then Peace.
And from the midst
A flower
White.
And one by one
The petals turned
Till they hung
Seven radiating flames.
And again
The petals fell away
And the calyx was upborne.
Silence
Peace
Mist
The return.

Love.
Not that bright Flaming-winged
But Very-love.


## PAGEANT

Silently, through the misted, silver quiet,
They come.
And the feet that were dancing,
And the music and laughter,
Are still.
And the wreaths that were
Of poppies and vine-leaves,
And the sheaves of wheat,
And the purple fruit of the vineyards
That they bore in their hands,
And the colored robes that they wore,
Were of one tint and transparence,
Silver.

And lightly they passed.
And music,
Long sought and forgotten music,
Lifted the mists.
And One, holding a scourge
Whose devious flames
Sang,
Bade them kneel down;
And each ineffable Victim
Went forth,
Bearing a golden, never-healing wound.


## IRIS

Ah, bow your head, white sword flower,
Lest you pierce the thing you would save,
Lest your white beauty slay me.
Let your heart's blue stain
Plead for my frailty.

## Walter Conrad Arensberg – Selections from *Idols* and *Others*

Pin:
water-pretzels

*Unusually for a serious writer, Walter Conrad Arensberg (1878-1954) was perhaps best known as an art collector during his lifetime rather than an art producer.   The son of a steel manufacturer, Arensberg spent the bulk of his adult life supporting various artistic causes with the help of his wife Louise.   His many books included* The Cryptography of Dante, *which posited Freudian interpretations of* The Divine Comedy, *and* The Cryptography of Shakespeare, *which claimed to reveal acrostics and anagrams of the name of Sir Francis Bacon, which was merely the tip of the Bacon iceberg. Arensberg was evidently unafraid to go into bizarre realms in the pursuit of his art, as further evidenced by his Avant-Garde poetry, featured not only in Imagist periodicals but also experimental venues like* 291 *and* TNT.   *His book* Idols *contains poems influenced by Symbolism and Surrealism and were among the most cosmopolitan and vivacious of verse featured in Imagist anthologies, proving that you can get away with just about anything as long it's a worthwhile anything.*

### VOYAGE A L'INFINI

The swan existing
Is like a song with an accompaniment
Imaginary.

Across the glassy lake.
Across the lake to the shadow of the willows,
It is accompanied by an image,
— As by Debussy's
"*Reflets dans l'eau.*"

The swan that is
Reflects

38

Upon the solitary water—breast to breast
With the duplicity:
"The other one!"
And breast to breast it is confused.
O visionary wedding!    O stateliness of the
procession!
It is accompanied by the image of itself
Alone.

At night
The lake is a wide silence,
Without imagination.

### AUTOBIOGRAPHIC

Permanently in a space that is anywhere here
While I am I,
I am temporarily
Always now.

And at the eternal
Instant
I look—
The eye-glassed I
At the not I, the opaque
Others,
Eye-glassed too.
And I who see of them
Only the glasses
Looking,
See of myself
In looking-glasses
Faces
Distorted.

And throughout the transparent
Spaciousness,
Which is so extensively

The present
Point
Located personally –
A solid geometry
Of vacancy
Bounded by the infinite
Absence,
I
Forshorten
To the end
Of me...
Walls and ceilings
Of my cellular
Isolation
Wrecked by perspective,
Habitable cubes
Of static
Surfaces of plaster
Prolonged in flight.
And it is I who hold them back,
And it is I who let them go,
These gray planes plunging
In an emptiness
Blue,
These rampant sides of pyramids
That converge
To nothing

While I am I.


## AT DAYBREAK

I had a dream and I awoke with it,
Poor little thing that I had not unclasped
After the kiss good-bye.

And at the surface how it gasped,
This thing that I had loved in the unlit
Depth of the drowsy sea...
Ah me,
This thing with which I drifted toward the sky.

Driftwood upon a wave,
Senseless the motion that it gave.


## THE VOICE OF ONE DEAD

Of the relented limbs and the braid, O lady,
Bound up in haste at parting,
The secret is kept.

## Adelaide Crapsey – Cinquains from *Verse*

*Though never a part of Imagism in her lifetime, Adelaide Crapsey (1878-1914) had a tremendous impact on the craft and atmosphere of American poetry – entirely after her death. The daughter of an Episcopalian minister who would eventually be thrown out of the church for heresy, Crapsey was highly active in her formative studies, including at the Wisconsin-based girls' school Kemper Hall, where she later returned as a teacher. During her academic career she began to suffer from tuberculosis, a condition that would eventually take her life at the age of thirty-six. Crapsey returned to poetry in her final years, a practice she had excelled at in school, and in an astonishing period of creativity invented a new poetic form, the cinquain. Modelled after ancient Japanese and Chinese poetic forms, cinquains were very brief, tightly controlled poems of five lines of increasing syllabic length, ending with a brief line to make a climactic point. Most of her poetry was published posthumously in a tiny volume of Verse by a small, theosophical press, and later was reprinted in an expanded form by Knopf to immediate acclaim and impact. The cinquain became a vogue among dozens of poets and has persisted to this day as one of the greatest formal creations in American verse, and Imagism counted it as a sister effort to everything they were attempting to encapsulate. Crapsey's own examples remain some of the most moving and effective metered poems in American poetry.*

### NOVEMBER NIGHT

Listen...
With faint dry sound,
Like steps of passing ghosts,
The leaves, frost-crisp'd, break from the trees
And fall.

## TRAPPED

Well and
If day on day
Follows, and weary year
On year...and ever days and years...
Well?

## SUSANNA AND THE ELDERS

"Why do
You thus devise
Evil against her?" "For that
She is beautiful, delicate;
Therefore."

## AMAZE

I know
Not these my hands
And yet I think there was
A woman like me once had hands
Like these.

## TRIAD

These be
Three silent things:
The falling snow...the hour
Before the dawn...the mouth of one
Just dead.

## MADNESS

Burdock,
Blue aconite,
And thistle and thorn...of these,
Singing, I wreathe my pretty wreath
O'death.

## FATE DEFIED

As it
Were tissue of silver
I'll wear, O fate, thy grey,
And go mistily radiant, clad
Like the moon.

## THE WARNING

Just now,
Out of the strange
Still dusk...as strange, as sill...
A white moth flew.  Why am I grown
So cold?

# CONVERSATION PIECES

The traditions of poetic structure have proven hell for those who value vernacular as a culture's chief form of linguistic expression. While free verse in America was initially inspired by Eastern and Ancient poetic forms, many writers quickly saw its potential for capturing American speech in all its peculiar splendor. The works of the poets in this section utilized this newfound elasticity to create ingenious prose-poems and character sketches, eschewing austerity in favor of empathy and storytelling.

*William Zorach's cover for* Mushrooms *by Alfred Kreymborg,*
*1916.*

## Alfred Kreymborg – Selections from *Mushrooms*

Pin:
Pierrot
with the hiccoughs

*Some artists have been hailed more as curators of the work of their colleagues than for their own work and still have drawn considerable praise for their oeuvres. Alfred Kreymborg (1883-1966) was one of those artists, and with more joyous passion than anyone before or since. Kreymborg spent nearly his entire adult life as an editor, founding several magazines and ongoing projects in dizzying succession, such as* The Glebe, Others *(which first assembled many of the figures here),* Broom *and* The American Caravan. *On top of this was his own poetic work, initially in the form of quirky, conversational verses that emphasized bouncing rhythms, speed and humor. These early tone-poems he called "Mushrooms", and his first book of poems was titled the same, being released in 1916 to wide acclaim. He extended his approach to drama, both for human actors and for marionettes, and was a founding contributor to the body of work that was produced by the Provincetown Players, America's first experimental theater venue. His free verse output evened off after* Mushroom's *follow-up,* Blood of Things, *but Kreymborg never stopped his support for modern American poetry, even in the face of personal obscurity.*

### SCHERZETTO

Stop, queer little dear!

Why is a kiss?
I don't know.
You don't?
No!
Then why do you do it?
Love!
Love?
Yes!

And why is love?
I don't know.
You don't?
No!
And why don't you know?
Because!
Because?
Yes!

Come, queer little dear!


## A SWORD

A million-bladed sword,
slashing the petty pates
and sticking the smug stomaches of the past
till the pink blood dribble
and, with a roar of ribald song,
a whirlwind of naked dance,
flaunting the laughing boyish present on a pike
against the stare and whisper of the doddering
future –
a sword is love!


## ROMANCE

That red-headed woodpecker, tapping my ear,
(Come out and see there!
What?
Over there!
Where?
Over there!
Yes, in the air.)
is seven songs fair
the peer of you all.
Beware?

I don't care –
I love him, the dear!

## ENTITY

I am.
And you.
And atoms.
Censure?
Forgiveness?
Why?

## THEOLOGY

The night is a circus tent.
The stars are peep holes
the bad ones have made
to spy on us.
Why aren't the gods like us?
Why don't they pay
and come in the way we did?
Are they poor?
Are they cheats?
Maybe they fear we'd make clowns of them?
Suppose we did;
aren't clowns the gods of our circus?
What's the matter with those fellows?
Tell them to climb down
and come in free.
We don't want them staring in on us.
It annoys the performers.

## PROGRESS

Quoth a god;

See them move,
slowly, serenely, onward,
through mountains and all,
stretching and dragging
their long steel bodies,
their slimy bodies,
rib by rib,
across continents,
and leaving their spawn,
cities,
behind them.
Egregious worms!

## DANCE

Moon dance,
you were not to blame.

Nor you,
lovely white moth.

But I saw you together.

## CHILDREN

They live; we exist.
They feel; we think.
They come; we go.

They play; we fumble.
They dream, awake; we dream, asleep.
They sleep; we toss.

We cannot be.
But let us try.

## CULTURE

There is only one.
Only one sun.
Only one moon.
And you too.
Be that.

## Jeanne D'Orge – Selections from *Others*

*Jeanne D'Orge ((1877-1887)-1964) wasn't born Jeanne D'Orge, but became her through will and love, and at great expense to her past lives.  Born Lena Yates in Cheshire, she followed Alfred Burton, then the dean of M.I.T., to Boston, in 1906, and by 1916 had reinvented herself as Jeanne D'Orge, appearing in* The Little Review *and* Others *with a series of elusive and alluring poems that synthesized verse and internal monologue.  Poor health brought her and her family to Carmel, CA, where she met Carl Cherry, a former student of Burton's, and by 1925 she had left her family for Carl, scandalizing her little community.  Nevertheless, she and Carl created a thriving artistic haven in Carmel, and D'Orge continued to write and refined her personal visions of nature and man in the presence of the Divine in paintings.  Her later poems would focus on natural awe and explore autobiographical content, using swift narrative verse to process her deep emotions about her tumultuous personal life.  While her earlier verse doesn't touch upon these subjects, the poems show a unique voice honing its craft.  D'Orge's philosophy was one of intense sympathy, depicting individuals struggling to find happiness in a world where magic is underfoot, and that humility to life's greater forces is affirming of humanity rather than detrimental to it.  Her work has largely only been reprinted in scarce limited editions, so the editor is proud to have a chance to reprint some of her most accomplished early poems.*

### STOLEN

I crept slyly
to your table
....Oo...m
Sugared peaches drowned in chianti...

Destiny
shaped heavily like a nurse girl
yanked me by the ear
planked me in my high chair.
"There," said she,

"Eat what is set before you,
Impudence."

Oh bread and butter
flat every-dayness
monotony
milk.

## PRAYER RUG

It is made of silences –
many colored silken threads –
the purple of various deaths –
red gold sacrifice –
meditation – a delicate green stillness
melting into blues of ecstasy.
These are the background
for one thread
that follows the mystic outline
of a cross –
and in the centre wreathed
seven red roses
seven fires of silence...
To pray
is to stand upon these
with naked feet
breast bare to the sun
and to sing.

## MATINS

The crust of sleep is broken
Abruptly –
I look drowsily
Through the wide crack.
I do not know whether I see

Three minds, bird-shaped,
Flashing upon the bough of morning;
Or three delicately tinted souls
Butterflying in the sun;
Or three brown-fleshed, husky children
Sprawling hilarious
Over my bed
And me.


## THE CONVENT

Nice to be God...
My passions sit in long white rows
within the little chapel
sending incense up to me
or fast singing in lonely cells
or walk whispering together thro grey cloisters.
Last night a wildcat novice broke her vows
and now her sisters wear away the stone
praying for her.
They cannot guess who slipped the bolts
    Who rose with her
    Who gave her to her lover...
        Nice to be God...


## THE ENCHANTED CASTLE

We climed to it by secret flights
of kisses...
When the door burst open
it vanished...
        Crash...
            Bump...

Earth again...
"What are they saying?"

"There's a baby coming…"
"He scuttled off on rat's feet…"
"The girl's in the ditch…"
"And the castle?"
"You don't mean to say
you believe that faery story?"

## BEFORE MEETING

There will be no shock
as of two strange sparks
suddenly fused;
no breathless pause
as when friends meet
after long absence.
It will be very simple
very easy.
The truth is already set to music.
There is only the singing.

## THE STATUE

I have left a song –
A strong cry of exultation
Standing under the dome
Of the Great Central.
A cry…a song…
A long white gesture of love
With upturned lyric palms
Held out to the people…
The nervous…hurried…weary…blind
          …deaf people
Passing…

## Ruth Suckow – Selections from *Poetry* and *Pagan*

*A native of Iowa, Ruth Suckow (1892 – 1960) is best remembered now for her many stories, published in major periodicals of the day, probing and reflecting small-town life in her Midwestern home state. After studying at the Curry School of Expression in Boston and later the University of Denver, she returned to Iowa and spent several years running an apiary, using her isolated, peaceful setting to begin writing. Her first published story appeared in 1921, and in that same year* Poetry *published a few of her poems; another would be included in the second* Pagan Anthology. *Her verses were few, and are now a virtually forgotten aspect of her* œuvre, *yet show how a young writer can use old forms, as well as experimentation with free verse, to empathize with the tough-and-tender American mood of her brethren. I apologize for breaking with the free verse format of this volume for most of this section, but I feel that if I don't reprint her poems, who will?*

### BEAUTY

I went where pines grew;
    Beauty I found in these,
In stars, and in the strange
    Twisted boughs of trees.

I went where houses were;
    Beauty I found then
In eyes, and in the strange
    Twisted lives of men.

### GRAMPA SCHULER

Grampa Schuler, when he was young,
Had a crest of hair, and shining eyes.
He wore red-flowered waistcoats,
Wild Byronic ties.
The whole land of Germany
Wasn't wide enough! –

He ran away one night, when winter
Seas were fierce and rough.

He has a sleek farm here
With already a settled air.
He's patriarchal, with his sons
And daughters round him everywhere,
His son's son Jim has fiery eyes –
He wants to go where the land is new!
Grampa bitterly wonders: "What are
Young fools coming to!"


## THE ODD ONES

I like best those crotchety ones
    That follow their own way
In whimsical oblivion
    Of what the neighbors say.

They grow more rare as they grow old,
    Their lives show in their faces –
In little slants and twisted lines;
    Like trees in lonely places.


## SONG OF LITTLE HINES

Little Hines, who mends watches.
Is writing an epic.

He has taken the universe for his theme
and calls it
*Man and God.*

He has a little shop with a gray front,
and there, in his work-room,
with a green-painted counter,

and watches hanging—like drying fruit—on a black
   cloth,
and pictures of dogs, cows, and Abraham Lincoln on
   the wall,
and a stove on a wrinkled tin plate,
he examines all day
the minute machinery of watches.

But at night,
in his closed back room,
his spirit examines
the vast and intricate workings
of the universe.
Miltonic angels sweep down about him
on great wings;
caverns of flame spurt and roar beneath him,
and there is a sound of harp-music.

These things he records on large white paper
with the water-mark of an eagle.

The soul of little Hines
has also written a lyric in my heart,—
all in a minor key;
and when I see pitiful gentle things—
violets struggling through a hard soil—
it sings and quavers in my heart,
grotesquely sweet—
a Marche Triomphale played on a cabinet organ,
wheezy and out of tune,
with the diapason sticking.

## Maxwell Bodenheim – Selections from *Minna and Myself*

> Pin:
> a tooth
> toe-dancing

*Many authors from this volume came of age as part of the Chicago Renaissance of the 1910's and 20's, a period of remarkable artistic production and vigor that won the city nationwide fame. Among the most colorful of the many, many writers to grace the streets of the Windy City in those years was Maxwell Bodenheim, (1892-1954) a native of Mississippi who would spend most of his working life in New York. A good friend of Chicago weirdo and screenwriter Ben Hecht, Bodenheim co-founded the* Chicago Literary Times, *which featured work by the likes of Carl Sandburg, Theodore Dreiser, and former* Spectra *pranksters Witter Bynner and Arthur Davison Ficke, among others. He moved to Greenwich Village in the '20's and earned international notoriety, eventually seeing his career collapse in scandal, and was ultimately murdered, alongside his third wife Ruth, in a flophouse on Third Avenue, during a period of homelessness. His work contains humor and sympathy for the downtrodden, without getting in the way of good satire, and never strays from natural cadences, designed as much as speaking pieces as printed texts.*

### TO A DISCARDED STEEL RAIL

Straight strength pitched into the surliness of the ditch:
A soul you have – strength has always delicate, secret
          reasons.
Your soul is a dull questions.
I do not care for your strength, but your stiff smile at
          Time:
A smile which men call rust.

## CHORUS GIRL

Her voice was like rose-fragrance waltzing in the wind.
She seemed a shadow stained with shadow colors
Swinging through waves of sunlight.
Perhaps her heart was an old minstrel
Sleepily pawing at his little mandolin.

## DEATH

I.

A fan of smoke in the long, green-white revery of the
sky,
Slowly curls apart.
So shall we rise and widen out in the silence of air.

II.

An old man runs down a little yellow road
To an out-flung, white thicket uncovered by morning.
So shall I swing to the white sharpness of death.

## POET-VAGABOND GROWN OLD

The dust of many roads has been my grey wine.
Surprised beech-trees have bowed
With me, to the plodding morning
Humming tunes frail as webs of dead perfume,
To his love in golden silks, the departed moon.
Maidens like rose-flooded statues
Have bathed me in the wine of their silence.

But now I walk on, alone.
And only after watching many evenings,
Do I dance a bit with dying wisps of moon-light,

To persuade myself that I am young.


## LOVE

You seemed a caryatid melting
Into the wind-blown, dark blue temple of the sky.
But you bent down as I came closer, breaking the
image.
When I passed, you raised your head
And blew the little feather of a smile upon me.
I caught it on open lips and blew it back.
And in that moment we loved,      \
Although you stood still waiting for your lover,
And I walked on to my love.


## FACTORY GIRL

Why are your eyes like dry brown flower-pods,
Still, gripped by the memory of lost petals?
I feel that if I touched them
They would crumble to falling brown dust
And you would stand with blindness revealed.
Yet, you would not shrink, for your life
Has been long since memorized,
And eyes would only melt out against its high walls.
Besides, in the making of boxes
Sprinkled with crude forget-me-nots,
One is curiously blessed if ones eyes are dead.


## TO AN ENEMY

I despise my friends more than you.
I would have known myself but they stood before the
          mirrors
And painted on them images of the virtues I craved.

You came with sharpest chisel, scraping away the false
        paint.
Then I knew and detested myself, but not you,
For glimpses of you in the glasses you uncovered
Showed me the virtues whose images you destroyed.


## DEATH

I shall walk down the road.
I shall turn and feel upon my feet
The kisses of Death, like scented rain.
For Death is a black slave with little silver birds
Perched in a sleeping wreath upon his head.
He will tel me, his voice like jewels
Dropped into a satin bag,
How he has tip-toed after me down the road,
His heart made a dark whirlpool with longing for me.
Then he will graze me with his hands
And I shall be one of the sleeping, silver birds
Between the cold waves of his hair, as he tip-toes on.

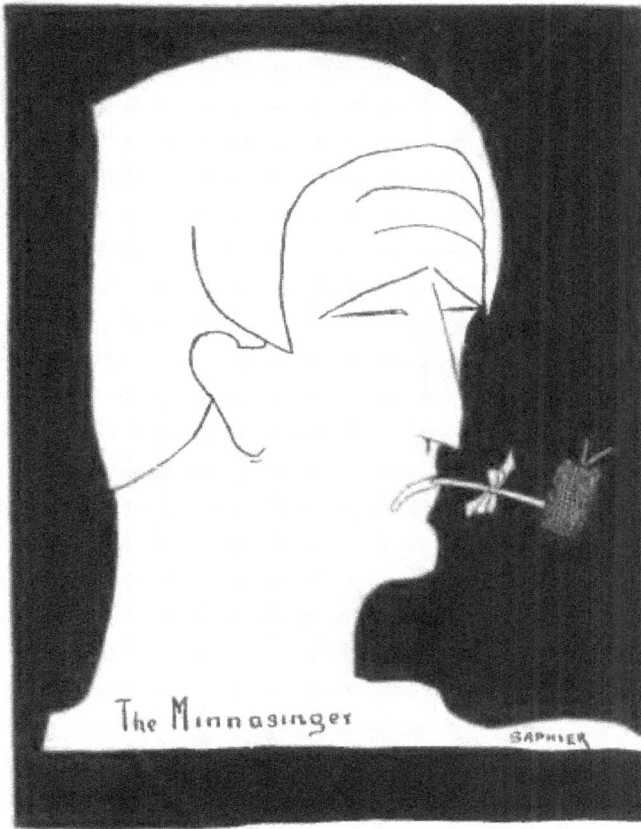

The Minnasinger

SAPHIER

*Caricature of Maxwell Bodenheim by William Saphier in* Pins for Wings, 1920.

# CIRCLING NEW YORK

*The heart of free verse was the little magazine movement, and the heart of the little magazine movement was, as so many of the writers included here prove, New York. Its stature as a center of culture, combined with its tremendous wealth and proximity to London, the birthplace of English modernist poetry, made it an artistic powerhouse which no other American city could outpace. The writers featured here, whether native or immigrants to New York City, made unique contributions to an artistic legacy that continues to grow to this day.*

## Baroness Elsa – Selections from *The Little Review*

*It may seem a bit of a cheat to include Else von Freytag-Loringhoven (1874-1927), the self-proclaimed "Baroness Elsa", in an anthology dedicated to American poetry. Born Elsa Plötz in Pomerania, the Baroness made her way to America after a serious of tumultuous relationships, her last, failed marriage leaving her as an artist's model in Cincinnati. Travelling East, she met her third husband, Baron Leopold von Freytag-Loringhoven, and the two settled in New York, where she began to unleash her artistic vision. Blurring the lines between life and art, the Baroness was among the first in America to create art from found objects, displaying assemblages as well as elaborate costumes that she modelled herself. She also published a slew of Dadaist poems in* The Little Review, *and her typographically daunting, impassioned verse sparked innumerable arguments in the "Letters to the Editor" section and baffled most of the magazine's readers. Only recently has her work been rediscovered, and here the editor has the pleasure of reprinting much of her work from* The Little Review *to baffle a new generation of readers. Perhaps the Baroness wasn't indebted to Imagism, but one can't deny that her English verse was a stunningly original contribution to American poetry of its day, the first (and some could argue the last) Dadaist verse in the U.S.A.*

### MOVING-PICTURE AND PRAYER

With the easy grace of a duke — a little too self-conscious —he disappears — chinless — behind the marblewall — leading to the lunch counter — —

*Now* I remember! He is the LUNCHCOUNTERMAN!

Vaguely I always hated him —
Today I hate him *distinctly*—so that it pains me not to abuse and kill him'

Ah — do you understand me — my pallidfaced reed — with the cynical droop of the lipcorners— eyes of devotion — never been devoted — or in being devoted — brought to tears — unwept?

Do not shift your eyes—here—there—*close* your eyes—for we are in America—not to get hurt—we must dream—dream—ah—If so possible not before the marble wall of a lunchcounter—

God I pray Thee —

### Metaphysical speculation—logic—consolation
### Concerning love to flame-flagged man

Know a man—red hair—
harsh mouth—harsh soul—
flesh hard white alabaster—
steely violet-blue shadows—
country of forbidding ice—
Every one fingertip must freeze to

touch

his deadly snowy waste.

Ah—why should EVERY ONE fingertip YEARN to touch a frozen body—AH—why should VERMILLION body yearn—ask—ask—yearn to smash adoring bones upon walls of castle of ice

Slippery it must be—I will glide—glide—WHERE TO—
A-H-H-H—WHERE TO?
This man's arm—will it melt into human muscle—flesh—into MASCULINE muscle—flesh—to save my so-adoring bones?
Or am I to become a corpse—vermillion still in death—affection oozing from me—enveloping him in death—freezing around him—wall of shimmering ruby blood—CRYSTALBLOOD?

Will he walk with shimmering wall of crystalblood around him—walk over my late adoring bones—pitiful mess—man—red hair—tender mouth—tender soul—palms of snowwhite shimmering hands full of emerald shadows—spices of passion—melting in first pathetic childlike gesture of contact—tremulous—hesitant—breathless smile

**67**

of unbelief—ecstasy flitting fitful painful—joyful over lips so recent accustomed to holy joy?

I answer my question:

Not dost belief—soul—in smashing of adoring bones.

AH-H—soul—! homeless wretched soul—pale—thin—naked—without jewels and feathers?

—Not yet has he taken me—not bedecked me with alabaster possessions!!!

I in space—body in sorrow and dust.
YET WILL I STEP INTO CASTLE OF ICE,—
adoring bones clinging to me—
—to be DRAGGED—
not to be smashed by glittering walls
glit-tering—wal-ls—cruel—splen-dor!
Into castle of ice I will step BY CONTACT—seering fluid
forcing passage into walls of no approach.

Inside glamour—.illumination—adoring bones smashed—STRETCHED by holy joy—adoring bones—smashed bones—tremulous bones—weak bones—NEVER BEYOND REPAIR!
FOREVER LASTING IN STRENGTH AND WEAKNESS—HIS AND MY ADORING BONES!

THERE IS A WIRE OF CONTACT IN THAT FLAMEFLAGGED CASTLE OF ICE.

A-H-H-WHAT ELSE IS LOVE—BUT ELECTRICITY!

HY—THE FLAG OF MIRTH AND PASSION AND JOY ON TOP OF THIE TOWER OF THE CASTLE OF JOY!

HAIR—HIS VERMILLION HAIR!!!

## KING ADAM

Thus will be thine orbs: filmy—with curtains of happiness—
Thine mouth—stern—harsh muscles of thine jaws relax in pain—sweet as tears.
Breathless—thine     heart—breathless—choking thine throat—

Back it will drop into thine chest pounding thine frame!.
Jugular vein behind thine vengeful ears—along thine vengeful
white neck—fly like sides of a bellows.
Flesh: crystal—transparent.
Crimson joy in thine heart—crimson thine orbs!
Soft rubber thine bones—weak thou art—child!
Brain leave thee—Blissful—leave thee—seconds eternity.
Thine sheen: brass—-copper—snow—scintillating moonstone—
Scin-  lat-   moonstone— — — —
     til-   ing

Saint Antony the second—wiser than first—
Sawest unity—necessity—sacrifice— — —Joy—
battle—death—life—Godsatan—Satangod—
Saint Antony the second— *Wise One*!

Adam—warrior—smile th strength—knowledge—
Adam—*New Man*—steppest *lightly*—friend of serpent—drowsiness gone—Adam—takest Earth!

Such mine love: electric fluid—current to thine wire—to make *Light*—Ah—h—h—such mine love!

Kiss me.........upon the gleaming hill.........*
Adam—Mine Love!
After thou hast squandered thine princely treasures into mine princely lap—there remains upon mine chest a golden crimson ball—weighing heavily—
Thine head—
          King Adam—Mine Love.


*Donated to the censor


**69**

## BUDDHA

Ah—the sun—a scarlet balloon
Ah—the sun—
—scarlet balloon
giant balloon
touching spires and steeples
down the misty grey—late
afternoon—
crystalline—late—
afternoon— — —
— — — —
vanishing
immense—
immune. — —
God:
scarlet balloon—
Everything simple!

Giant balloon—
God—!
vanishing—
immense—
immune—
eye on us—
on *Himself!*
*Circle!*
Sufficient!
*Most importantly round!*
Withal: space!
Fact.
Gay God—scarlet balloon.

Gay God—scarlet balloon.

*Round!*
Deed—joy:
*Round!*

Perfection!
Who is he—
crowds *thee*
wiith responsibility!
Gay God—scarlet balloon?

Whirring God—immense in sky

Lightness—
emptiness—
out of
heaviness!
material to
immaterial!
Ether—soul—
fliest:
touching spires and steeples—
down a misty grey—
—late afternoon—
crystalline—late—
afternoon— — —
— — — —
vanishing
obscure
immune—
*Essence!*
Whirring God—immense in sky.

Ah—soul—scarlet balloon—
Ah—soul—
Soul—scarlet balloon—
giant balloon—
touching spires and steeples—
down thy misty—grey—
afternoon—
crystalline—
afternoon— — —
— — — —

balancing—
immense—
immune—
soul—scarlet balloon
Everything simple!
Ah—Mustir—scarlet balloon—
giant balloon—
Ah—Mustir—simple!
Touching spires and steeples
down thy misty—grey—dim
afternoon—
crystalline—dim—
after — —
noon —

## HOLY SKIRTS

Thought about holy skirts—to tune of " *Wheels are growing on rosebushes.*" Beneath immovable—carved skirt of forbidding sexlessness—over pavement shoving—gliding—nuns have wheels.

Undisputedly ! since—beneath skirts—they are not human! Kept carefully empty cars—running over religious track—local—express—according to velocity of holiness through pious steam—up to
heaven!

What for—
what do they unload there—
*why do they run?*

Senseless wicked expense on earth's provisions—pious idleness—*all* idleness unless idleness *before action—idleness of youth*!

Start action upstairs—he?
How able do that—all of sudden—when on earth—machinery insuffient—weak—unable to carry—virtuous?

72

Virtue: staganation.
Staganation: absent contents—lifeblood—courage—action! action-
n!

Why here?
What here for—?
        To good? ah—!? hurry—speed up—run amuck—jump—
beat it! farewell! fare-thee-well—good-bye! bye!
ah—bye-ye-ye!

We—of this earth—like this earth!
make heaven here—
take steps here—
to possess bearing hereafter—
*dignity.*
That we know how to enter:
reception room—drawing room—
banquet hall of:
*abyssmal serious jester*
*whimsical serene power!*
Poke ribs:
old son of gun—
*old acquaintance!*
Kiss: knees—toes!
Home—!
Our home!
We are home!
After:
smiling grim battle—
laughter—excitement—
swordplay—
sweat—
blood— — !
After accomplishing—
what sent for to accomplish.
Children of His loin—
Power of power.

## APPALLING HEART

City stir—wind on eardrum—
dancewind: herbstained—
flowerstained—silken—rustling—
tripping—swishing—frolicking—
courtesing—careening—brushing—
flowing—lying down—bending—
teasing—kissing: treearms—grass—
limbs—lips.
City stir on eardrum—.
In night lonely
peers—:
moon—riding!
pale—with beauty aghast—
too exalted to share!
in space blue—rides she away from mine chest—
illumined strangely—
appalling sister!

Herbstained—flowerstained—
shellscented—seafaring
foresthunting—junglewise—
desert gazing—
rides heart from chest—
lashing with beauty—
afleet—
across chimney—
tinfoil river
to meet
another's dark heart!

Bless mine feet!

# BLAST

Take spoon—scapel—
Scrape brains clear from you—
how it hurts to be void!
blast flew
over twin hillocks
emeroyd.
singeing—seering satanic stink—
flew—blew—
blushroses!
barren grew—
to you—
annoyed
protruding
sharp:
pointed pyramids
silence—drums—
—sphinx—
I smother—
pranked mother—
from stark things! ! !
stark kings in rockchamber
mockeye set amber
within mine chest! ! !
to rest—
no!
ripple—glide—quiver:
Nile
river!
overflow!
hillocks inundated
abated
blush
blushroses!
on twin hillocks
smaragd isle!
awhile—awhile—!

## MOONSTONE

Lake—palegreen—shrouded—
skylake—clouded—shrouded—
yearning—blackblue—
sickness of heart—
pomegranate hue—
sickness of longing—
—! you!

In cloud—nay—ach—shroud—
nay—ach—shroud—!
of—breast—
sickness of longing
gulps
pomegranate hue
from heart in chest—
palegreen lake in chest!
— you!

## IS IT?

It is—is it—?
heart white sheet!
kiss it
flame beat!
in chest midst
print teeth
bite— — —
this green
ponderous night.

## Orrick Johns – "Ebb Sand and Stars"

> Pin:
> the Rubaiyat
> carved on a carrot

*A contemporary of Edna St. Vincent Millay, Orrick Johns (1887-1946) is often remembered for entering, and winning, the same poetry contest that Millay entered her famous long poem "Renascence". He would later say that the magazine was in error in giving him the prize over her. A native of St. Louis, Johns moved to New York when his first poems brought him notice, and spent much of his career in the service of left-wing institutions, editing* New Masses *and taking part in many WPA projects. While his most Avant-Garde work in poetry and drama is contained in his second book,* Black Branches *(1920), including three memorable "plays in chiaroscuro", his best work in the editor's opinion is to be found in his first book,* Asphalt *(1917), which dazzles in its diversity of approaches and humanistic conscious. Most of its work is traditionally metered, including the title set which uses a purposefully ignorant vernacular voice to explore the difficulties of working-class existence, but the final pages feature some of the most effective free verse of the late 1910's, closing with this haunting set of fragments, eerie and austere in their construction and imagery.*

I.

From that last touch of fingers
The broken wire,
The message suspended
Over a desert of rain.

II.

Peace...go,
And in strange places,
Unexpected turns,
You will find me.

III.

Unforgotten?
Unremembered?
Does the river forget light
Or remember flowing?

IV.

Here,
There will be sounds always
Of music beginning...
Born of that anguish.

V.

Better to bless
Those steeps of yourself,
Those flowered valleys,
With new grass.

VI.

Peace...go...
Ah no...come closer,
Yes...go,
You cannot help come closer.

VII.

Ebb sand and stars,
These be the healing mutes...
Beaten down are the sounds of the sea,
And I am alone...

VIII.

The tree will whisper,
The window laugh,
The room hold me...
Trying to displace you.

IX.

Yes, the wheat and the tares,
The able and pitiable things...
The sky of my memory of you
Floods them all.

X.

I would go deeper
But I fear to tread the earth there,
I fear that crust.
There is all hell beneath it.

XI.

And the nights,
They will be filled with lines,
That vainly try to express longing,
While the wind flaps a shutter.

XII.

O temple bells!
O far Japan of that verandah!
Such grief will come
From a spiral vine with flowers...

XIII.

The sumach will follow you,

The plum-bloom and redbud,
And the flowers of another summer...
But I shall not feel good-bye.

XIV.

These things that I say
They will be as nothing
They will be as dead grass
They will be burnt up with flame.

## Routledge Curry – "An Orchid"

*As time and tide have proven that the printed word long outlasts its author, occasional authors have less evidence of their existence preserved in publication than their peers and uncovering their identities can prove very difficult. Routledge Curry is a name without a life, as research on my part has revealed not one speck of biographical information; as far as can be discerned his posthumous reputation rests upon his sole published poem, "An Orchid". Published by the Pagan magazine in their first* Pagan Anthology, *it is unknown by the editor if the poem appeared in the magazine itself or only in this book. Pagan's second-tier status among magazines that were already below the radar gave it a peculiar knack for attracting figures who came from, and returned to, nowhere. Regardless of its history the poem is an effective cousin of Imagist techniques, and the editor would be interested to see if Curry developed his style any further. We can only guess if he was an interloper to verse publication or merely unlucky, but his lone surfaced work is more than deserving of reprinting.*

The old mahogany fireplace
Had an ample cloth of dark green velvet
Over its mantlepiece.

On it
I placed a slender silver vase,
And filled it with a solitary orchid
Of rare beauty.

The peacock flower
Possessed a soft shy face,
And it rolled quaint scarlet kisses
To me
Down curious paths of lavender and gold,
Trailing its eager, graceful petals
To a point.

## William Saphier – Selections from *Others*

*Born in Romania, William Saphier (1886-1942) better known as an illustrator than as a writer, with his work appearing in both sumptuous books like his deluxe* Book of Jeremiah, *and in fleeting goofs like "Emmanuel Morgan"'s* Pins for Wings, *where he caricatured many of his fellow artists. The main outlet for his poetry was* Others, *for which he served as associate editor. Don't think that this means that his verse was of a lesser quality – far from it, in fact, and the refinement and sheer invention of these poems suggests a talent far beyond what little work of his made it to print. Like so many poets featured here there is no collected edition to help us, and one for Saphier's writing is long overdue.*

### MOOD

The end of my wish
Walks near me smiling;
With subtle fingers I loosen
Little shining, sharp chips
From the crystal body
With its many enticing shadows.

A fine silk thread
Is desire,
These sweet but sharp edges
Its end.
Shall I add one more flaw
To my dream veil.

### FLAMINGO DREAMS

A green and copper-backed frog
keeps me from seeing
brick-colored eucalyptus flowers
dancing on an apple-green sky;
large rose-hued cotton fists

82

with gold knuckles
chase a blushing sun
into a purple, lead sea:
I am hungry and he is cautious.

## MEETING

Her glance swung my body
like a bell
in a long forgotten church
and the tingling emotions came forth
like sounds, summoned,
at attention,
grouped around an altar
of a great love.
Stiff like a bronze pillar
I came
and drank the two tears
her eyes offered
like raised crystals
at a solemn farewell meeting.

## RAIN

Like crawling black monsters
the big clouds tap at my window,
their shooting liquid fingers slide
over the staring panes
and merge on the red wall.
Some of the fingers pull at the hinges
and whisper insistently: "Let us come in,
the cruel wind whips and drives us
till we are sore and in despair."
But I cannot harbor the big crawling black clouds,
I cannot save them from the angry wind.
In a tiny crevice of my aching heart

there is a big storm brewing
and loud clamour and constant prayer
for the reflection of snow-capped mountains
on a distant lake.
Tired and dazed I sit on a bear skin
and timidly listen to the concert of storms.


## MARGRETHE

You are an ice covered twig
with a quiet, smiling sap.
The spring winds of life
have tested your steel-blade soul
and the harsh breath of men
covered you with a frigid shell.
But under the transparent ice
I have seen your warm hand
ready to tear the shell
and grasp the love-sun's heat,
and your cool morning eyes
look clear and calm into the day.

## David Rosenthal – "Cornbread and Eyes"

*A deeply obscure figure, David Rosenthal (fl. c. 1917-1927) has defied biographical research. A frequenter of New York's left wing circles, including* The New Masses, *Rosenthal skipped his way through various periodicals of his day before vanishing into thin air. His work is uneven in quality, but a couple of his poems shine like gems. This pair of miniatures, published in 1922 in* Broom, *striking at the heart of everything that made Imagist-era free verse so exciting – mystery in clarity, getting right to the point of evocation.*

I.

When the candle dies,
Darkness will rush in,
Like wolves
Upon a carcass.

II.

Before a tree may learn to stand,
It first must walk the fields
And mountains
In a seed.

## Evelyn Scott – Selections from *Precipitations*

Pin:
candied colon

*A native of Tennessee, Evelyn Scott (1893-1963) is best remembered for her many novels, such as the historical drama* The Wave *and her fictionalized memoir* Escapade, *as well as her love affairs with Waldo Frank and William Carlos Williams. She was also the author of two books of poetry,* Precipitations *(1920, her first book) and* The Winter Alone *(1930), both severely neglected in critical appraisals of her work. Her verse deserves far more attention than it's gotten, as it applies free verse technical tricks to dark, surrealist ideas. Like Frances Gregg, she has been dismissed as a companion to great writers than a great writer herself, which has kept her poetry from returning to print. This dismissal is concerning, as I can't think of another poet of Scott's time with the same command of imagery, psychological insight and flair for using words to keep twisting the knife of nightmare into a reader's mind.*

### VENUS' FLY TRAP

A wax bubble moon trembles on the honey-blue horizon.
Softly heated by your breast
Pearl wax languorously unfolds her lily lips of mist,
Swells about you,
Weaves you into herself through each moist pore,
Absorbs you deliciously,
Destroys you.

### GUITARRA

"An orange tree without fruit,
So am I without loves,"
His heavy lidded eyes sang up to her.

Her glance dropped on her golden globe of a breast,
And on the baby.

## THE TUNNEL

I.

I have made you a child in the womb,
Holding you in sweet and final darkness.
All day as I walk out
I carry you about.
I guard you close in secret where
Cold eyed people cannot stare.
I am melted in the warm dear fire,
Lover and mother in the same desire.
Yet I am afraid of your eyes
And their possible surprise.
Would you be angry if I let you know
That I carried you so?

II.

I could kiss you to death
Hoping that, your protest obliterated,
You would be
Utterly me.
Yet I know – how well! –
Like a shell,
Hollow and echoing,
Death would be,
With a roar of the past
Like the roar of the sea.
And what is lifeless I cannot kill!
So you would make death work your will.

III.

In most intimate touch we meet,

Lip to lip,
Breast to breast,
Sweet.
Suddenly we draw apart
And start.
Like strangers surprised at a road's turning
We see,
I, the naked you;
You, the naked me.
There was something of neither of us
That covered the hours,
And we have only touched each other's bodies
Through veils of flowers.
But let us smile kindly,
Like those already dead,
On the warm flesh
And the marriage bed.

IV.


The blanched stars are withered with light.
The moon is pale with trying to remember something.
Light, straining for a stale birth,
Distends the darkness.

I, in the midst of this travail,
Bring forth –
The solitude is so vast
I am glad to be freed of it.
Is it the moon I see there,
Or does my own white face
Hang in blank agony against the sky
As if blinded with giving?

V.


Little inexorable lips at my breast
Drink me out of me

In a fine sharp stream.
Little hands tear me apart
To find what they need.

I am weak with love of you,
Little body of hate!

## THE LONG MOMENT

A white sigh clouds the fields
Into quietness.
Above the billowed snow
I drift,
One year,
Two years,
Three years.
Hurt eyes mist in the blue behind me.
The moon uncoils in glistening ropes
And I glide downward along the dripping rays
To a marble lake.

# *SPECTRA* AND AFTER

In 1916, a mysterious book was published entitled *Spectra: A Book of Poetic Experiments*. As Imagism was still quite new, critics took the book's claims to "push the possibilities of poetic expression into a new region" as wholly serious. This was not the case, and the hoax was eventually unmasked, much to the embarrassment of the greatest champions of the Spectra "school". Three poets claimed the title of Spectrists: Emmanuel Morgan, Anne Knish and Elijah Hay – whose real names were Witter Bynner (1881-1968), Arthur Davison Ficke (1883-1945) and Marjorie Allen Seiffert (1885-1970), respectively. Their experiment was to spoof current trends in modern poetry with the hope that critics would take the bait, and while they succeeded the hoax had a curious secondary effect. Aside from Ficke, whose non-Knish work never rose above mediocrity, the "legit" poems of Bynner and Seiffert were heavily influenced by their time under the guise of satire, and their follow-up books to *Spectra*, *The Beloved Stranger* and *A Woman of Thirty*, display the best fruits of that influence. In each poet's case, they would never again achieve the resonance and formal excellence of their immediate follow-ups to *Spectra*. This section collects the best Spectrist verse along with the most accomplished free verse from after the curtain had drawn, to see if the hoax can become reality and succeed.

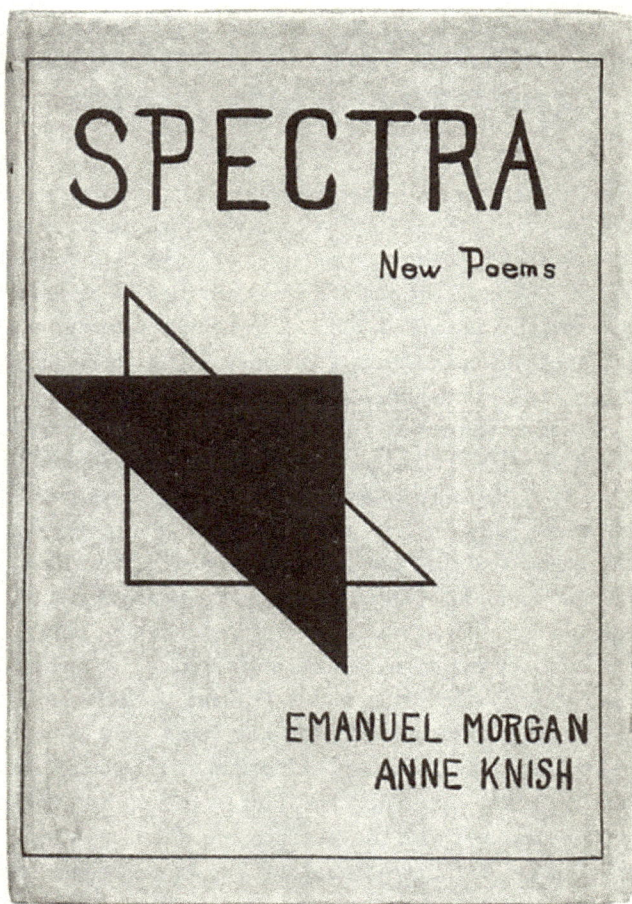

*The cover of* Spectra, *1916.*

**Witter Bynner** writing as **Emmanuel Morgan** in *Spectra*

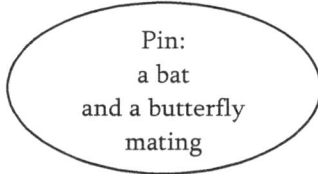

> Pin:
> a bat
> and a butterfly
> mating

### OPUS 7

Beyond her lips in the dark are a man's feet
   Composed and dead…
In the light between her lips is a moving tongue-tip
sweet,
   Red.

Her arms are his white robes,
  They cover a king,
His ornaments her crescent lobes
  And two moons on a string.

*Sheba, Sheba, Prosperina, Salome,*
  *See, I am come! – king, god, saint! –*
*With the stone of a volcano O show that you know me,*
  *Pound till the true blood pricks through the paint!*

Twitch of the dead man's feet if he remembers
   A bunch of grapes and a ripped-open gown.
And the live man's eyes are night after embers,
  Two black spots on a white-faced down…

And in the dawn, lava…rolling down…
Downrolling lava on an up-pointing town.

## OPUS 2

Hope
Is the antelope
Over the hills;
Fear
Is the wounded deer
Bleeding in rills;
Care
Is the heavy bear
Tearing at meat;
Fun
Is the mastodon
Vanished complete...

And I am the stag with the golden horn
Waiting till my day is born.

## OPUS 40

Two cocktails round a smile,
      A grapefruit after grace,
Flowers in an aisle
      ...Were your face.

A strap in a street-car,
      A sea-fan on the sand,
A beer on a bar
      ...Were your hand.

The pillar of a porch,
      The tapering of an egg,
The pine of a torch
      ...Were your leg,

Sun on the Hellespont,
      White swimmers in the bowl

Of the baptismal font
                Are your soul.


## Witter Bynner – Selections from *The Beloved Stranger*

Pin:
God
in the sugar-bowl

### VEILS

This veil
Of lavender and dawn
Floats off
Invisible,
And this purple noon
Unwinds in wisdom,
And this of evening
Twitters, undulates,
Dips, darts,
And this of night
Circles around me singing
To the very edge and presence of the young
                moon –
And it brushes the tip
Like lips
Three times.


### LIGHTNING

There is a solitude in seeing you,
Followed by your company when you are gone.
You are like heaven's veins of lightning.
I cannot see till afterward

How beautiful you are.
There is a blindness in seeing you,
Followed by the sight of you when you are gone.

## HORSES

Words are hoops
Through which to leap upon meanings,
Which are horses' backs,
Bare, moving.

## CRYSTAL

Between your laughter and mine
Lies the shadow of the sword of change.

Yours is innocent.
Mine knows.

You had sat abstracted
By the touch of dreaming strings
Of an old guitar –
When in the centre of the room
A crystal dish cracked for no reason.

Then you darted with joy to the fragments,
Like a fish to a crumb,
And held between your thumbs and your fingers
Two pieces of laughter.

## A GHOST

You leaned against me,
Humming a slow song
Of purple shadows...
Showers and javelins and shooting-stars

Fell through me where you leaned...

Whose ghost was I?


## TOUCH

Someone was there...

I put out my hand in the dark
And felt
The long hair
Of the wind.


## FLAME

Is it your fault
That winds from heaven sweep through me and
        I call it you?
Is it your fault
That the chin and throat of you are the curve
Of a mountain-brook where I would drink,
That your whole body is a heap of stinging sweet-
        ness from the pines,
That when you sleep your silence is an arch of the
        moon, your motion thunder of the moon,
And when you wake your eyes are the long path
        of ocean to a new burning,
To a nest of phoenixes
Whose golden wings
Are tipped with flame?
Is it your fault
That phoenixes arise from fire –
And dragons?

## PEACE

When I am crucified upon his brow,
Will the strange god be at peace?

**Arthur Davison Ficke** writing as **Anne Knish** in *Spectra*

Anne Knish Pin:
a gargoyle
remembering

Arthur Davison Ficke Pin:
St. Sebastian
in gloves
trimming his arrow-tips

## OPUS 118

If bathing were a virtue, not a lust,
I would be dirtiest.

To some, housecleaning is a holy rite.
For myself, houses would be empty
But for the golden motes dancing in sunbeams.

Tax-assessors frequently overlook valuables.
Today they noted my jade.
But my memory of you escaped them.

## OPUS 182

"He's the remnant of a suit that has been drowned;
That's what decided me" said Clarice.
"And so I married him.
I really wanted a merman;
And this slimy quality in him
Won me.
No one forbade the banns.
Ergo – will you love me?"

## OPUS 191

The black bark of a dog
Made patterns against the night.
And little leaves flute-noted across the moon.

      I seemed to feel your soft looks
Steal across that quiet evening room
Where once our souls spoke, long ago.

      For that was of a vastness;
And this night is of a vastness...

      There was a dog-bark then –
It was the sound
Of my rebellious and incredulous heart.
Its patterns twined about the stars
And drew them down
And devoured them.


## OPUS 200

If I should enter to his chamber
And suddenly touch him,
Would he fade to a thin mist,
Or glow into a fire-ball,
Or burst like a punctured light-globe?
It is impossible that he would merely yawn and rub
And say – "What is it?"


## OPUS 150

Sounds, pure sounds –
Nothing –
Vibrancies of the air

And yet –

      This summer night
There are crickets shrilling
Beyond the deep bassoon of frogs.
They cease for a moment
As the rattling clangor
Of the trolley
Bumps by.
I hear footsteps
Hollow on the pavement
Now deserted
And blank of sound.
They die.
The crickets now are sleeping;
Even the leaves grow still.

      And slowly
Out of the blankness, out of the silence,
Emerges on soundless wings
The long sweet-sloping
Rise and fall of far viol notes, -
The mad Nirvana,
The faint and spectral
Dream-music
Of my heart's desire.

**Marjorie Allen Seiffert** writing as **Elijah Hay** in ***A Woman of Thirty***

Pin:
lather
but no beard

## SPECTRUM OF MRS. Q.

Fear not, beautiful lady,
That I shall ravish you!
Your arms are languorous lilies –
There is not a thorn
In all your slender greenness,
And you are sweet to madden buzzing bees!

Fear not, beautiful lady,
A hard, black cricket
Inspects you.


## A WOMANLY WOMAN

You sit, a snug, warm kitten
Blinking through the window
At a storm-haunted world –

Sleet wind caterwauls
Through icy trees,
Which clack their hands at you
Tauntingly.

Why should you leave
Radiator and rubber-plant?
Do people stand at attention to mourn a hero
When they behold
A frozen kitten

In a gutter?

## NIGHT

I opened the door
And night stared at me like a fool,
Heavy dull night, clouded and safe –
I turned again toward the uncertainties
Of life withindoors.

Once night was a lion,
No, years ago, night was a python
Weaving designs against space
With undulations of his being –
Night was a siren once.

O sodden, middle-aged night!

## Marjorie Allen Seiffert – Selections from *A Woman of Thirty*

Pin:
in a bath-tub filled
with Pierian springs
she washes off her
inhibitions with a
gurgling elbow

## SEQUENCE

I. "Arrival"

Shining highways
Sing to your step,
Windows beckon,

Doorways open a square embrace.

Doors laugh gently
Swinging together
Behind you.

II. "The Tower"

There's a flag on my tower,
And my windows
Are orange to the night.
They are set in grey stone that frowns
At the black wind.

Inside, there's a guest at my hearth,
And a fire
Painting the grey stone gold.
My windows are black
With the hungry night peering through them.

Blackness lurks in corners,
Wind snatches the sparks,
Tongs and poker jangle together
Like the iron bones
Of a man that was hanged.

III. "They Who Dance"

The feet of dancers
Shine with mirth,
Their hearts are vibrant as bells:

The air flows by them
Divided like water
Cut by a gleaming ship.

Triumphantly their bodies sing,
Their eyes are blind

With music.

They move through threatening ghosts
Feeling them cool as mist
On their brows.

They who dance
Find infinite golden floors
Beneath their feet.

IV. "Pianissimo"

I took Night
Into my arms,
Night lay upon my breast.

If night had wings
She would have brought me
Stars for my hair.

The stars laughed
Lightly
From far away.

About my shoulders
White mist curled.

V. "Portrait by Zuloaga"

Death lies in wait
For those who do not know
What they desire,
And hell for those
Who fear what they have taken.

These hands are wrinkled
From stretching forth,
Brown

From the winds blowing upon them.

They are strong with seizing,
They do not tremble.

VI. "Gestures"

Let there be dancing figures
On our wine-flask,
Swastikas on our rug,
Inscriptions in our rings
And on our dwelling.

Let us build ritual
For our worship,
Pledge our love
With vows and holy promises.

If oaths are broken,
Let it be darkly
With threatening gestures.

Thus we ignore
That we love and die
Like insects.

VII. "Veils"

I shall punish your blindness
With a veil.

I shall choose words that join
Gaily word to word,
I shall weave them flauntingly
Into veil upon veil,
I shall wind them defiantly
Over my lips, over my eyes.

You shall not see your name
On my lips,
You shall not see your image
In my eyes!

And through my veils I shall not see
That you are blind.


VIII. "Freedom"

I would be free
From two old superstitions,
Thanks and Forgiveness.

So I would think of you
As Flame,
As Wind,
As Night,

To whom I have been
Wind,
And Flame
And Night,

Together burned and swept,
Now smothered
In separate darkness.

IX. "Mud"

I am dazed and weary
From the shapelessness
Of what I am –

I am poured
Among haphazard stones
In meaningless patterns.

Yesterday's sun dried me
Between rounded cobbles,
Today's deluge sweeps me
Toward alien pavements,
Tomorrow's sun shall dry me
In a new design.

Better the turbid gutter
Toward the open sea!

X. "Fools Say –"

November's breath
Is black in the brances of trees
And under the bushes,

Harsh rain
Whips down the rustling dance
Of leaves.

There is smoke
In the throat of the wind,
Its teeth
Bite away beauty.

Let fools say:
"Spring
Will come again!"


## THE LAST ILLUSION

Along the twilight road I met three women,
And they were neither old nor very young;
In her hands each bore what she most cherished,
For they were neither rich, nor very poor.

In the hands of the first woman
I saw white ashes in an urn,
In the hands of the next woman
I saw a tarnished mirror gleam,
In the hands of the last woman
I saw a heavy, jagged stone –

Along the twilight road I met three women,
And they were neither fools nor very wise,
For each was troubled lest another covet
Her precious burden – so they walked alone.


## THE PATHWAY OF BLACK LEAVES

I. "The Turning"

The pathway opened before her eyes
Between black leaves –
She laughed, and shivered, and turned aside
From the dusty road.

Her feet moved on like heart-beats,
She could not stop them;
Relentlessly each step fulfilled itself
And the steps behind it –
A hidden chain, drawing her onward
Captive.

And yet she said: "Now I walk free
At last!"

II. "Toll-Gate"

The sign read:

"Paupers may pass untaxed,

The Rich shall pay a penny,
The Poor
Must give all they possess."

She emptied her pockets bravely and passed through...
They gave her a golden coin in return for her silver,
Bearing on one sidethe head of a king,
And on the other a worn inscription
Curved like a wreath
And written in a tongue she did not know.

III. "The Inn"

There was the inn, beside the path,
Standing like the words of an ancient prophet
Forgotten long, now suddenly come true.

"They who break bread here
Shall not eat for hunger;
They who lie here
Shall not sleep."

All night long the black leaves, one by one,
Laughed, and shivered, and fell into darkness.

IV. "Return"

She has come home
To the house she knew:
But she has forgotten
The square oaken smile of the door.

The room is a stranger,
The fire is sullen;
On her hair a black leaf shines
And clings where it fell.

Against her heart

She has hidden away
The bitter golden profile of a king.


## DISILLUSION

I touch joy and it crumbles under my fingers –
The dust from it rises and fills the world,
It blinds my eyes – I cannot see the sun.
A choking fog of dust shuts me apart.

I remember the sparkling wind on a bright autumn
    Morning,
I let down my hair and danced in the golden gale,
Then chased the wind chased fallen
    Leaves –
Wind cannot be caught and tamed like a bird.

I touch joy and it crumbles to dust in my fingers.

# INTERLOPERS

It's easy to forget that modernism wasn't born in a vacuum, and the energies that brought poetry authors together and into production caught artists from innumerable other fields into its swirl. The poems featured here were all written by people deeply involved in other endeavors, including school administration, painting and political activism.

## Henry Bellamann – Selections from *A Music Teacher's Note Book*

*Best remembered as the author of* Kings Row, *a scathing indictment of small-town Midwestern life a là* Main Street, *Henry Bellamann (1882-1945) spent most of his adult life as a music teacher, serving as the Dean of Curtis Institute of Music and de facto director of the Juilliard School of Music, as well as heading the music department at Vassar College. During this time he was somehow able to write three books of poetry, all in free verse and all long out of print. His critical neglect is puzzling to the editor, as his work shows great versatility and achievement for someone who eked it out as a hobbyist. His decades of musical experience informed his poems, many of which are sketches after contemporary Classical music – an uncommon practice in verse in which he may have exceeded the attempts of his peers, even Lowell's from earlier in this anthology.*


### A STUDY

> Strindberg was right,
> And William Blake,
> And Freud, perhaps –
> Consider this fantastic scheme:
> School,
> The English room,
> "Exams", -
>
> I watch your red-gold head
> (Such a lot of hair!)
> Bending over the desk.
> Sometimes you look up
> And tap your teeth
> With the pencil rubber,
> Sigh and think.
>
> On the board is chalked:
> "Trace the development of the English novel."

## MACABRE

The moon is old:

> Her eyes are white like horn,
> And blind.
> She toils along an age-old way,
> Forgetful of the world's young dawn,
> Forgetful of the ancient songs,
> And deaf to new.

The moon is cold:

> Her icy track
> Lies white across the lake.
> Your lips are pale and frozen
> In that light –
> Your face – moon-cold,
> Moon-dead.

The moon is mad:

> She is in flight
> Before the ghosts
> Of things that never were.
> She would destroy –
> Her hands are seeking
> For my eyes – my heart!

The moon is old and cold – and mad.


## ABOVE BATTLE

I wonder if the souls of men
Met up there in the Flanders fog,
If they knew the way.

# DEBUSSY

I. Prelude

A silver dragon,
Slender as a reed,
Wakes from his sleep on a lacquered tray
And drops his length,
Shining coil on shining coil,
Among the gray-green leaves
Of a tiny garden
Patterned on a tabletop.
Poising his carved and lustrous head,
He delicately intones
A slow, fantastic monologue.
Crystal cold and thin
The ancient measures flow,
While a dragon-fly,
Perched, like a painted eagle,
On a pygmy pine,
Listens in silence.
A passing swallow
Hurls his shadow on the garden's elfin lake –
The dragon-fly takes sapphire flight,
And the silver dragon
Climbs to his vermilion tray
To sleep.


II. Jardins sous la pluie

Rain,
Like waving threads of raveled silk,

116

Curls across the window glass
And breaks the picture of the garden
And the flowers
And the fountain
And the little black pagoda
Into a quivering kaleidoscope.
The wind bells
Shiver under the beating clappers of the rain.
And the long green vines
With purple blossoms
Shake from the trellis
Like inverted fireworks.
Under the eaves
A cheerless bird complains,
And a little lost wind
Goes among the leaves
And sings a song about the stars.


III. Clair de lune


A flower moon,
Tall stemmed above a bank of clouds,
Stands in the east;
Some fallen petals of her light
Float on the sea.
Mellow gold notes
From a mandolin
Sound outside an ancient wall
On which dark lichens
Mold an apograph
Of legends carved on stone.
Behind the high, heraldic gates
A tracery of leaves,

Stiff and precise,
Conceals a faun
Who dances to the mandolin,
And wriggles his furry ears,
And grins.

(IV.) La terrasse des audiences du clair de lune

The dark
Filled with muffled sounds;
Rustle of silk,
Soft tap of canes,
Exclamations of polite surprise,
And the exquisite staccato
Of murmured French.
Colored globes,
Deep in the crowded trees,
Reveal the flutter and hurry of preparation.
The rising moon,
Hung in a turquoise arch,
Gilds the terrace
Of waiting audience.

From far, high towers
Comes the unhurried,
Uncadenced
Chiming of bells.

(V.) Feux d'artifice

Ah!
Wheels of sparks –

Green,
Red,
Darting blue!
Chain and lattice and lace of light!
Fringe and spangle and fret of fire!

High above the gulf of black,
The curving flight
Of rockets
Blossoms in a shower of white and sudden stars.
Fading jewels of fairy gift –
Fire-drake dancing with Will-o'-the-wisp,
And – dark.

(VI.) Minstrels

A drollmouthed minstrel
In tattered black and red
Struts round the cathedral corner.
A girl
Leans from the balcony in the Rue des Ponts,
And listens to his cynical strumming.

Freedom sings on the lute-strings –
Sings of the sunny road to Provence,
And the tavern fire;
Hints of two-edged jests,
And wine-warm kisses
Of .... .... just such a red-lipped boy
As he, whose graceful leg
Struts round the cathedral corner
In tattered black and red.

Tuba mirum .... .... spargens sonum,

Rolls in Gregorian solemnity
From old St. Louis en l'Ile,

Coget omnes ante thronum,

And drowns irreverent couplets,
Sounding still
Down the Quai d'Anjou.

Liber scriptus proferetur

The girl in the balcony
Suddenly closes her eyes,
And sighs.

(VII.) Cloches a travers les feuiles

Golden tents
Are pitched upon the wide, blue plain;
Temple gongs
Sound across an ecstasy of light,
The vista
Leads beneath the painted torii
To the golden tents
And the perfect mountain.
Shall we go
And lift the silken doors of tents,
Or shall we pluck the scarlet poppy-petals
Here?

## Ernestine Hara Kettler – "Modern Art"

*Modernism in the 20th century was frequently a partner, and sometimes venue, of left-wing political movements, such as Socialism and its many shades. Women's suffrage was reaching a fever pitch at the same time that free verse came into its own in America, but overlap was unusually sparse. A briefly involved, but well-remembered Suffragette, Ernestine Hara Kettler (1896-?) dipped a toe into poetry with "Modern Art", a single poem included in the first* Pagan Anthology. *Much like Routledge Curry's single poem, "Modern Art" more than merited inclusion in this anthology, and it would be interesting to see if more has survived – one can never know what may turn up.*

### MODERN ART

Arms awry
Legs astride . . . .
This jumbled mass
Of humans
Sprawling
On the green.

What demons
Set them
Rolling,
Stumbling,
Falling crazily
Over each other
Like a stupid mess
Of kittens
Rolling downhill
To a picnic? . . . .

## Marsden Hartley – Selections from *Others* and *Poetry*

*One of America's finest Cubist painters, Marsden Hartley (1877-1943) took great inspiration from his experiences in Europe during the first World War, as well as the writings of Whitman and the Transcendentalists. A friend of Kandinsky's, his earliest work combined abstraction with Expressionistic themes. He returned to the U.S. in 1916 he travelled the country, painting gorgeous landscapes in Massachusetts, New Mexico and his native Maine. A little-known part of Hartley's output are his poems, many of which reflect his view that art was a spiritual quest, and pay special attention to light, landscape and the textures of human yearning.*

### GIRL WITH THE CAMELIA SMILE

Eyes –
          Little vanity mirrors
From Damascus.
Her hair –
               Is a packet of love-letters
Burned to a crisp – on the Sunday
Morning – of a sad young man.
Gowned one way – a maple leaf
Bitten with frost-lips –
Whisked from the last boughs
                              Of October.
The last wild leaf fierce with autumnal ecstasies.

He was one wind who danced with her –
The sad young Sunday-morning man.
He had seen her – gathering –
                         Shell-flowers
On a brown sea's edge –
Before the moon had withered.

## SALUTATIONS TO A MOUSE

If a mouse makes a nest
Of one's written words,
Is there else to do but accept
The flattery?
I have deemed it wise to do so.
I have thanked him
Sufficiently
As he scurried in and out
Of the room.
He has faced the winter
With a nest of my words.
I did not suspect them
Of such worth against the cold.


## EVENING QUANDARY

There is water flowing
      From the padre's garden.

There is water flowing
      Under the solid gate.

There is water flowing,
      Wat – er.

Drip, drip, drip, drip,
      From the padre's garden.

It is not raining.
      The stars are all laughing.

There is water flowing,
      From the padre's garden.

Ten o'clock in the evening,

From the keyhole.
Drip, drip, drip, drip, drip.

If it had rained today,
I would say it is the patter of sky feet
In the padre's garden.

There is water flowing,
From the padre's garden –
Everywhere.


## SYNTHESIZED PERFUMES AND ESSENCES

Morning comes with such rapidity, purple plum
hanging onsensuous boughs over my head,
sweeping my shoulders, grazing my cheek,
that I wonder one ever thinks of the going
of evening.
I never talk of evening save to say of it, it is another
kind of light.
Dark holes called doorways are for me only as
places to go into where one watches the
light of night from them.

Danse l'Aigle – L'homme Rouge.  As we watched
him swinging and descending, we saw the
dew of multiple benefactions dropping
from his wings.  In this beak he held
fragments of the morning gathered from
the lips of the red cliff nearest the sun of
dawn.
How splendid he is, the lady from the fiord
remarked.  I stroked his wings and felt the
warmth of the centuries on my hands.  It
emphasized our infancy in point of time.
It emphasized our vacuity in point of
experience.

124

There is room on the housetops for love.  There is
            room over the housetops for the moon to
            rise and resume the old eloquence.
If there is anything for lovers in the rising of the
            moon, they will be welcome to the
            supposition.  The sky has time for nothing
            but approval, of all things, that are trivial.

Against the long thin sky of our willfulness, there
            hangs the marriage pear.  If brown hands
            with to make a syrinx out of olive boughs,
What is the objection?  The wood is oiled for
            music.  Someone will be in love with
            someone, despite a certain prejudice.
The weevil falls to dust with every suit of clothes.
            If the gem is hard, it is rather sure of
            retaining its accustomed radiance.

Water running beside my bed.  The brook brought
            to my bedside.
The little pool, when the tide is out.  Anemones
            and crabs at home.
Violet and orange.  Indian orange.  Roseate, ashy
            gold.
Seaweeds made of torments rolling out of brown
            eyes.
Froth from the tossed wave.  My bedlinen shall be
            made of it.
The window nearest my bed shall be made of
            forsaken cusps of the moon.
I shall sleep, with an orange, a lemon, and an
            avocado on a little table.

A silver plate with the red seeds of the pome-
            granate divested of their juices.  A
            pampas plume shall wave with the breath

of nightingales from a distant orchard. I
think I could care for such a sleep. For
once, at least.

## TO C—

I.

If a clear delight visits you
Of an uncertain afternoon,
When you thought the time
For new delights was over for that day,
Say to yourself, who rule many a lost
Moment in this shadowy domain,
Saving it from its dusty grey perdition,
Say to yourself that is a flash
Of lightning from a so affectionate west,
Where the clear sky, that you know, resides.
The rainbow has crossed the desert once again.
I took the blade of bliss and notched it
In a roseate place.
It shed a crimson stream —
That was our flush of joy.

II.

They will come
In the way they always come,
Swinging gilded fancies round your head.
So it is with surfaces.

They will walk around you
Adoringly,
Strip branches of their blooms for you —
Young carpets for young ways.

With me it is different.

126

Stars, when they strike
Edge to edge,
Make fierce resplendent fire.
I have lived with bright stone,
Burned like carnelian in the sun.
Myself;
Myself seen branches wither.

Carbon is a diamond –
It cuts the very crystal from the globe.

You are so beautiful
To listen.

I WALKED IN TO
A MOMENT OF GRE
ATNESS. THERE WAS
A WAVE OF PURE EM
OTION RUNNING THRO
UGH THE AIR—LIKE A PU
LSE RECORDING THE BEAT OF
SOULS. I STOOD AGAINST A WALL,—
THE HOUSE WAS IN DARKNESS, LIGHT
ON THE STAGE, —THE LAST ACT OF
MEISTERSINGER HAD BEGUN. I LISTENED.
ALL OF ME HEARD. IF THAT STRAIGHT
LINE OF TERRIFIC TENSITY WHICH STRETCHED
CONTINUOUSLY BETWEEN MYSELF AND THE MUSIC,
—GROWING MORE AND MORE SENSITIVE EACH MO
MENT,—COULD HAVE EXISTED INDEFINITELY UNTIL THE
LINE BECAME INSEPARABLE WITH THE STATE ABOUT IT—
WHAT WOULD HAVE HAPPENED?
                    EVERYTHING HAD MERGED—THERE WAS NO
POSSIBILITY OF ANY RETENTION OF THE SEPARATENESS OF A HU
MAN SELF FROM THE SPACE OF SOUND INTO WHICH THAT SENTI
ENT SELF HAD PROJECTED. AN EXTENSION OF FEELING AND A DIF
FUSION OF MUSIC WITH IT—CREATING A CONDITION OF ONENESS. A
PASSING OF EACH INTO THE OTHER.
                    SOUND, GIVING,
                    WILL, FEELING,
                    AN INSISTENT ENTITY REACHED.
             WAS THERE ANY PART OF ME THAT DID NOT RESPOND?
I WAS NOT A WOMAN—I BECAME MERELY A PART OF THE ATTUNEMENT OF
THE MOMENT—AS DID ALL THE OTHERS. THE STRANGERS STANDING SO
NEAR THAT I COULD HAVE TOUCHED THEM—AND I THINK WE WERE TOUCH
ING. WE HAD DROPPED OUR LITTLE SELVES—WE WERE NOT— BUT
SOMETHING GREATER THAN OURSELVES WAS BREATHING. WHAT
GAVE IT THE IMPETUS TO BREATHE? AND IF IT COULD HAVE EN
DURED—IF A CLIMAX COULD HAVE BEEN REACHED AND HELD
FOR THE FRACTION OF A SECOND—WOULD NOT THAT I
NSTANT HAVE BECOME INFINITE? WOULD IT HAVE
BEEN DEATH? OR ESCAPE—INTO A QUICKEN
ING OF LIFE?

Katharine N. Rhoades

April 7—1915

Agnes Ernst Meyer

Small wonder that our knee-bent made a god
To shield them from this dimly heard
Daemonic laughter

But if the course of nature is obstructed
By her own clouded skies,
What then?

Then hope comes beckoning—and is crushed,
When I remember that the cool and dew-pearled morn
Is wakened, warmed—and soon made ready for its parched end
By any blazing sun.

*Katharine N. Rhoades's untitled poem in* 291 *no.3, May 1915.*

# Katharine N. Rhoades – Poems from *291*

*Many artistic figures in New York were linked by the incredible influence of the International Exhibition of Modern Art, later dubbed the Armory Show – the first major show of Avant-Garde painting, sculpture and photography in the U.S. Alfred Stieglitz was a principal organizer of the show, and a great friend of many of the poets in this anthology. Among his personal muses was the painter and model Katharine N. Rhoades. As a model Rhoades stood for Francis Picabia and Stieglitz's own work, and her own work was displayed in the Armory Show and Stieglitz's 291 gallery. She also had a major hand in* 291, *a periodical Stieglitz published that lasted for seven issues before folding. Each issue was highly experimental, tossing painting, photography prose pieces and poetry together into a joyous haphazardness, and among these pieces were three poems by Rhoades, her only published work in the genre. Built to take advantage of* 291'*s large page format, the poems pull no punches in reference to emotional candor and direct images, forcing the reader to confront their ideas head on – the raw experience being the greatest of truths.*

## NARCOSIS

Black spots

           moving

                      walking


      scattering
A million insistent centres at conflict
Countless forces and counter forces
         walking . .
         walking . .
         endlessly walking . .
Interminably dull yet irresistibly hypnotic
         a narcotic
Dull monotonous thuds and endless motion of
men.

Within – without –
Whirling antagonisms

dissipating

destroying
Perpetual motion
Light
Bulk
Lesion
Need
Cohesion?


**(UNTITLED)**

I WALKED IN TO A MOMENT OF GREATNESS. THERE WAS A WAVE OF PURE EMOTION RUNNING THROUGH THE AIR – LIKE A PULSE RECORDING THE BEAT OF SOULS. I STOOD AGAINST A WALL, - THE HOUSEWAS IN DARKNESS, LIGHT ON THE STAGE, - THE LAST ACT OF MEISTERSINGER HAD BEGUN. I LISTENED. ALL OF ME HEARD. IF THAT STRAIGHT LINE OF TERRIFIC TENSITY WHICH STRETCHED CONTINUOUSLY BETWEEN MYSELF AND THE MUSIC, - GROWING MORE AND MORE SESITIVE EACH MOMENT, - COULD HAVE EXISTED INDEFINITELY UNTIL THE LINE BECAME INSEPARABLE WITH THE STATE ABOUT IT – WHAT WOULD HAVE HAPPENED?

EVERYTHING HAD MERGED – THERE WAS NO POSSIBILITY OF ANY RETENTION OF THE SEPARATENESS OF HUMAN SELF FORM THE SPACE OF SOUND INTO WHICH THAT SENTIMENT SELF HAD PROJECTED. AN EXTENSION OF FEELING AND A DIFFUSION OF MUSIC WITH IT – CREATING A CONDITION OF ONENESS. A PASSING OF EACH INTO THE OTHER.

SOUND, GIVING,
WILL, FEELING,
AN INSISTENT ENTITY REACHED.

WAS THERE ANY PART OF ME THAT DID NOT RESPOND?  I WAS NOT A WOMAN – I BECAME MERELY A PART OF THE ATTUNEMENT OF THE MOMENT – AS DID ALL THE OTHERS.  THE STRANGERS STANDING SO NEAR THAT I COULD HAVE TOUCHED THEM – AND I THINK WE WERE TOUCHING.  WE HAD DROPPED OUR LITTLE SELVES – WE WERE NOT – BUT SOMETHING GREATER THAN OURSELVES WAS BREATHING.  WHAT GAVE IT THE IPETUS TO BREATHE? AND IF IT COULD HAVE ENDURED – IF A CLIMAX COULD HAVE BEEN REACHED AND HELD FOR THE FRACTION OF A SECOND – WOULD NOT THAT INSTANT HAVE BECOME INFINITE?  WOULD IT HAVE BEEN DEATH?  OR ESCAPE – INTO A QUICKENING OF LIFE?

### FLIP-FLAP

A man at a piano – thousand assembles, close, elbows touching.
　　　　Waiting.
　　　　　　　Manufactured Soul-stuff for those who
dare not create –
　　　　　　　Come and have your emotions played
upon!
　　　　　　　You like to suffer – so?
　　　　Hush……
　　　　A Sound!
　　　　Ah!
　　　　He plays – you hear?
　　　　Flip-flap….
　　　　All's forgotten –
　　　　　　　Emotions gyrate in the heavy air, keeping
time with the
　　　　　　　whirl and swirl of perfectly poised tones.

　　　　　　　Sound and sound and sound…….
　　　　Rippling –
　　　　Flip-flap.

131

An instrument making sounds, and we the sounding boards!
Laugh loud – Soul – if you have content.

Why this devastating repression?  Can't you laugh? – This noise is
terrific –
He is thundering out that bass – doing his best –
And the others?
All intently listening...............to their own feelings!

                           (We are great! we men of

inner response)


But you – Soul – could you laugh, yours would be the miracle –
Chopin and Schumann against your laugh!
                    Why don't you?
Can't you see yourself standing here looking down upon these
cringing, countless, round heads, and shapeless – and hair upon hair
– and hats – and heads again – ?
All these million eyes would look –
Every living man, even he who plays – would listen – and marvel –

                    Where's that laugh?
                    The music fills the house!
                    Louder! louder!
                    He pounds at the climax!
                    C sharp – he slipped – I cannot breathe –
                    Even the air has turned to sound!
                    They are applauding!  Soul!!
Because he finished – because you did not stop him –
He smiles – he almost laughs!
                    Endless noise and hands clapping –
                    A buzz of words –
                    I'm stifled – done for –

He seems quite calm himself –
He has gone beyond his finger-tips to feed these heads with his
inner darings –

He doesn't look much of a man – yet all these souls are flapping and turning
and beating and yearning –
        No laugh yet?  Soul of me – why not?
        To break into this orgie – into this maze of sound
and tensity –
        - where tuned-up Beauty flatters some few
hundred humans, and
        Lends them a vitality for this infected Now.


        Why mock the Artist? the Art that does the trick?
the thing
        That stirs and sighs?
                    What's a laugh
to that?

A Laugh! Such as this would be – could I laugh now!
Out into this sea of dreadful stutterings I'd throw an inversion – a revision –
Fool!
      A Whole Self – laughing –
      Yes, all – only my body dead – left here –
        Flip-flap –

        But the laugh?

Suppose they didn't feel a life there before them – laughing –
Didn't know just what a soul sounds like –
        Could I ever stop?

                            Who's laughing?

# OTHER HORIZONS

The 20th century saw an astounding democratization in the publishing industry in America, with the founding of presses dedicated to fine literature in cities across the country. However, New York held overwhelming influence as the hub of critical Standards and Practices, as it does to this day. The large volume of magazine verse from all corners of America prompted book publication in their authors' home cities, aided by the vogue of private presses and improved printing techniques. This section focuses on works by authors active outside of Manhattan. While the Boston-based Robert Alden Sanborn and Ohio State University professor Royall Snow were anomalies in verse publication, the authors from Chicago were members of the city's vibrant artistic boom during the 1910's and '20's, which also fostered Carl Sandburg and Maxwell Bodenheim. With recent publication trends that favor pluralism in art history, cities will reveal their hidden literary gems from this vital period in American literature.

## Ben Hecht - "Three Flesh Tints"

*Ben Hecht (1894-1964) will live forever in the history of cinema as one of the most revered screenwriters of the 1920's and '30's. His Hollywood œuvre included roughly seventy films, and it's perhaps no surprise that a writer of such prolificity began his career with enormous productiveness and variety. Hecht was one of the most original talents to emerge in Chicago in the 1910's, heading up a boom in artistic productivity that remains a fascinating and surprising body of work. Hecht's circle of friends included Maxwell Bodenheim, the extraordinary illustrator Wallace Smith and the important publisher Pascal Covici before he moved to New York. It was with Covici that Hecht created two singularly unbelievable novels,* Fantazius Mallare *(illustrated by Smith), concerning the decadent adventures of its title character, and its follow-up* The Kingdom of Evil *(illustrated by Anthony Angarola). These novels were an attempt to make shocking decadent works in the spirit of European Symbolist efforts, such as the illustrations of Aubrey Beardsley and the novels of J. K. Huysmans. Much of Hecht's other fiction, such as several stories and prose-sketches first published in* The Little Review, *as well as the set of three poems here, "Three Flesh-Tints", were similarly motivated. Symbolism never made much of an impact in the U.S.A. (aside from a pair of late-19th-century oddballs, Francis Saltus and Vincent O'Sullivan), so Hecht's dark, ambiguous exoticism was both unprecedented and never to be repeated. And in a similar spirit to Crane's* The Black Riders *there is a sense behind it all of laughter at God, or at least at our futile attempts to believe in a rosy version of reality.*

### "The Incense Burner"

A bending flower rises from its mouth
And sways like the vein of a zephyr.
Threads of moonlight float entangled over it,
Delicate as the breath of a dying woman.
Souls come whispering from its ancient lips,
Laden with thin secrets,
And torn by the long nails of idiot Gods . . .

Pale dancers arise, whirling listlessly.
Expiring in a writhing languor.
Heavy-lidded eyes crawl out and open vacantly
and close .
Dried whisps of water break into blue wings.
A sleeping woman's arm reaches up and curves into
a sigh
And scratches at the air with opalescent claws.
Dead pearls drift in a dead circle—till, quivering,
A slow finger rises, balancing a grey moon on its
tip.
And then a severed face squeezes out and lolls to
and fro,
Its washed purple lips leering with a grotesque sin.

### "The Goldfish in a Bowl"

A tiny shimmering courtesan
Dressed in red spangles,
Weaves a monotonous thread of painted rubies
Through the stagnant curtains of her room.
Stifling under faint rags,
A dumb enchanted nightingale
Tosses in droll anguish,
Dreaming of the sapphire roses and the crystal
fringe and the topaz silks
That were her lovers.

### "A Nude"

The rich brocade of night.
Sewn with the red dust of roses
And the topaz breath of the sleeping sun
Hangs from the cool ivoried silk of her shoulders.

The winged beacons of her breasts
Gleam with golden moonlight.
And her eyes are like purple bosomed birds

That circle and beat against the azure gloom.

Her nakedness is an opal mirror.
Quivering with splintered images.
Her nakedness is a white kiss.
Burning on the shadowed lips of the night.
Her nakedness is the flowing of ghostly water
Under fierce moons—
The poplar silver of the wind that dances in the gardens at night.

Her nakedness is the golden fabric woven out of bloody grapes
And the dead mists of incense.

## Mark Turbyfill – Selections from *The Living Frieze*

*Mark Turbyfill (1896-1991) was a remarkable man, distinguished as a poet, a dancer and choreographer, and a painter. While he was most famous for his dance career his poems started his artistic life and established him as a vital member of Chicago's artistic elite in its interwar boom. Among Chicago poets he was perhaps the most closely aligned with Imagist ideals, favoring concision in language and antique, exotic imagery. His most ambitious verse work was the proto-Science Fiction verse drama* A Marriage with Space, *published in* Poetry *in 1926 and later turned into an opera by the modernist composer John J. Becker, though to this day it's never been produced. His earlier poetry is his most comprehensible and was collected in* The Living Frieze, *published in 1921 in a gorgeously bound limited edition by Monroe Wheeler, a future fixture and publisher in the American expatriate scene in Europe in the 1920's. I hope that reprinting some of them here may spark a renewed interest, however modest, in the work of this modern Renaissance man.*

### THE ADVENTURER

Gatherer of shells,
Flower-hunter,
Breather of slight winds –
There is much to surprise me.
I bring you songs for flutes,
And odd-shaped leaves
And pointed vagaries.

These trinkets you may toy,
And twine into your moods –
Carelessly.

But I cannot tell you of what they are made
Or where I found them.

## COUNSEL

Beetle!
Draw in your toes
Lest the hoarfrost
Stringently
Tickle them.


## MELLOW

These soft hours,
The color of blurred pebbles
And wan sand,
Are an old worn fringe
About the breasts
Of the mellow afternoon.

The lilac lake
Is a saucer – thin –
Burdened with faint blue rings.

The brown velvet dog
Is a curved attitude
Upon the lawn.

Jagged in the black tree-lines
The frayed sun languishes –
A pale pink poppy
Grown too large.


## WITHOUT CHAPERON

Frail,
The white moon leans
To the green-edged hill.

The aspen lifts
Its tracery
Into light.

The moon slips down
The edge of night.

It is odd
To stand here alone –
This quaking aspen
And I.


## BATON

In the doorway
The little birds sit
Keeping time
To their thoughts.


## MEZZOTINTS

I.

Slanting
Yellow-gray dune.
Drenched with soft night,
Press against the opaque sky!
Across your throat
Swings one bursting star.

II.

I saw
With dream-strained eyes,
As at the world's yonder end,

A tarnished haze
Tawny as my furthest dream.
But seeking there again,
Soft on the breast of the night-drenched dune
Lay the flushing cheek
Of a persimmon moon.

## THINGS NOT SEEN

The sea-gull poises
In the charged, expectant air.

The sea-gull poises
With delicate resistance.

Its sheer conscious being
Is cause to strike creation
Out of all this emptiness.

The sea-gull waits,
Wavering slightly
Against this mighty immanence.

So does my heart wait
For the release of a substance
Not yet seen.

## SORROW

Step down, O night, with the
peace of indistinctness, that my
hnds need no longer hide my face
from the slow, slow day.

## THE FOREST OF DEAD TREES

I climbed up the rough mountain-side
Through the forest of dead trees.

I touched their smooth, stark limbs,
And learned much of the white beauty of death.

Whose taut, slender thigh was this?
And this, whose gracious throat?

O Life, you are not more beautiful
Than this silent, curving death is beautiful!


## A BOY'S SONG

His voice was soft,
Like the wondering, honest eye
Of a wild-wood deer;
He sang with the gladness of
Plum trees in bloom.
He had not in the voice of a man,
Nor of a woman –
His voice was brown
Like the breast of a meadow-lark.
The spirit of a lighter world
Tinted and fluted his song.
His notes knew something of wind
In soaring white clouds,
And something of pale green light
Which cinctures the moon
When she is shy.
For the voice of a boy
Is a passing dream,
And on his waking
Rises to the stars
Whence it came.

## Royall Snow – Selections from *Igdrasil*

*A longtime faculty member of the English department of Ohio State University, Royall Snow (1898-?) quietly produced a curious and compelling body of verse, enraptured by classical and ancient cultures and exuding a lush miasma of strange beauty. Snow edited* Youth: Poetry of Today, *a Cambridge, MA based periodical that attempted to bring together accomplished traditionalists such as Edwin Arlington Robinson with exciting new faces such as Witter Bynner and Malcolm Cowley. His goals here were crystalized in his own verse, published scantly in* Pagan *as well as the Boni & Liveright "subscribers only" book series* Poetica Erotica. *The majority of his verse appeared in his only book of poems,* Igdrasil, *published in 1921 by The Four Seas Company of Boston, one of the most adventurous publishers of verse outside of New York to get wide distribution in the 1910's and '20's. In the introduction of* Igdrasil *Snow explained that the name of the book came from the Yggdrasil of Norse mythology, a tree that draws water from three "Norns" representing the past, present and future respectively. His approach to free verse was to play with the flexibility that it allowed while retaining a "melodic" feel. The results of his ambitions were both accomplished and resonant.*

### IN A SECLUDED STUDY

The log fire
Is infinitely tender.
It combs the dark with smooth fingers of light,
It tries to warm the cold night
With soft kisses,
And when the night does not respond
It dies.

# CITY SKETCHES

I. Flirtation

Sluggishly the city
Draws her head back of a fan of night mists
To hide her yawns, while with her thousand eyes
She coquettes lazily with the river.

II. Lese Majeste

Somewhere off in the distance
A playful church spire sticks the full moon in the ribs,
And sends it spluttering indignantly across the sky
Like a stout burgher.

III. Gossip

One tall building.
Its base entangled in a cluster of squatty ones
Like a pencil stuck in a jar of peas,
Stares superciliously about;
The short buildings pretend scorn
And whisper catty things with their rattling
windowpanes.

IV. Vista

Across the river
The city makes a purple bas relief
Against an orange west.

V. Grotesque

They built that house of orange stucco
And gave it greenish blinds for eyelids
Either side the nose-like door.
It's a hobgoblin, halloween face

And it winks over the street at a church.

Heigh-ho, but the spinster church
Is very proper!
See her gather the trees
Like skirts about her.
And pretend to see only the stars!

VI. Corner Romance

His soul was like a trolley car:
Jolly, rumbling,
And eminently practical.
Hers was a httle pool of water that reflected the stars.
And then one day his soul came clattering down the
    street
And ran over hers.
Now hers reflects the stars no more
For his stirred up all the mud beneath.

### EXISTENCE

The notes
        Of the distant
                Piano
Were as butterflies in a far field:
One I caught
As a thousand drifted palely away.

And so with the world that whirls past:
Rich lips in a subway; a laugh
That trickles through a dark theater;
Black hair loose on white shoulders
While a shade is being drawn.

Meanwhile the dust rubs from the wings
Of the butterfly I have caught
And the others are flown.

146

## CONCERNING THE EGO

I. The Pearl-Diver

I plunge,
A sharp streak of bronze,
Through the sea-green chaos of my mind
To discover deep-drowned pearls.

II. On a Train

My heart is a tiger lily
Of fire blossoming;
It holds up the wavering cup
Of its golden eagerness
To the stars
Of an opening future.

And yet I am burned with it;
Years will pass before I see again
The tasselled cornfields of my native state.

## TRUTH

She had told him that she did not love him.
The laugh which he dropped scornfully at her feet
Was brittle
So that it snapped and cracked
In many places.
If she had lied, saying
That her life was a broken flute without him,
He would have kissed her.
And believed.

## Ruth Clay Price – Selections from *Pagan*

*Little is known about Oakland native Ruth Clay Price (1889-?), one of the first Californians to get modernist poetry published alongside Northeastern peers. After publishing some pieces in small Californian journals, she was featured in both of the* Pagan *anthologies – not that this acceptance into the Avant-Garde led to increased fame. She may have contributed to* Stuff: An Anthology of Verse, *a curious volume containing small poems on inconsequential topics, all signed with initials (and possibly also featuring work by Winifred Waldron, a fellow* Pagan *author). She may also have been writing in Oakland as recently as 1961; no notices of her death were found. Price was equally adept at metered and free verse, frequently experimenting with form to create unusual effects and amplify her quirky sense of humor. She was also one of the first poets to adopt the cinquain form after Crapsey. The editor is disappointed that none of her verse has been collected, and hopefully more information will come out of the woodwork on this elusive talent.*

### EYES

Seen from the balcony, looking down: -
    At tables around the dancing floor
    The midnight crowd is watching
    The stupid cabaret.


    Applause.
    Glasses clink.
    Louder the music sounds.


A                           dancing!
    beautiful           is
        girl

Flower –                   face.
    like          painted
       her

Cigarette smoke dims the room.
Men and women seem but eyes agleam,
Eyes, glancing at

The                                                                    dancing.
        girl                              is
                    who


                    Passionate thought eyes,

Leering,                                                        jeering!
                    sneering,

        A circle of concupiscent eyes
        Aglitter through the smoke.


## TRAMPLERS

    Elephants
    trampling the jungle:
        Monkeys,
                aloft,
                        jabbering frantically;
        the boldest
                hurling
                        ineffectual cocoanuts.
    Events
    trampling the world:
        individualists,
                aloof,
                        jabbering frantically;
        the boldest
                hurling
                        ineffectual protests.

# IMPRESSIONS

The virent salt-marsh tide is high to-night,
Rippling, swishing through the reeds,
The plashy, marshy weeds,
That flash of white, a homing gull in flight;
Some call it heeds;
Hush!

Trembling, the light recedes, the colors die,
The sky is gray, the shadow of night
Falls black on the water's light.
The heaven's deepen with stars, the wind glides by,
Night seems to sigh,
Hush!

Through space, from purple sky, the starlight falls
On pungent, lisping waves and grasses;
Night's magnetism passes
Through the marsh: a distant sea-bird calls,
The white mist crawls.
Hush,
Sh!

# ANTICIPATION

Pine tree:
Sun still,
Blurring the hill;
Thin growing,
Wind blowing,
Scent sowing;
Fulfill!

## Robert Alden Sanborn – Selections from *Horizons* and *Others*

> Pin:
> back-scratchers
> in bloom

*Robert Alden Sanborn was a man with two literary homes, anchored in Boston and most loved in New York. Educated in Cambridge, MA, Sanborn cut his teeth as a journalist before entering Kreymborg's* Others *circle. Sanborn wrote poetry as well as deftly revealing articles on the little magazines of his day, chiefly about Kreymborg and the importance of his corralling and broadcasting his collection of young free versers. He was one of the first people to recognize that the brief reign of* Others *and other little magazines of those years was a golden moment in American verse, with a mood and harmonious collection of talented voices never to be heard again. Sanborn's journalistic background may have contributed to the range and spirit of probing curiosity that defines his verse, shown in full splendor in his first collection* Horizons, *published in 1916 by the lovely Four Seas Company of Boston. His subject matter covered a wide span, from penetrating sketches of contemporary urban life (as in "The Fight") to word-painting verging on surreal abstraction (as in "Mauve"), all crafted with a fine eye for precision of detail and untroubled flow. Among the modernists Sanborn was one of the most cosmopolitan, reconciling old words and new techniques with remarkable grace and authority.*

### THE CROWD

I moved amongst a concourse crushing,
And everywhere I looked faces pressed upon me;
Their eyes did not look at me,
They were staring to see what I myself was seeing.
They did not see me, they moved upon and over me;
And I was afraid.
Many feet were upon me and the eyes were not seeing

me;
The feet did not feel me.
And I sank beneath the flood,
Bodies flowed over me;
And I sank yet deeper, and sinking, I died.

I died into passion,
Into sea beneath sea of stagnant passion
Passion of possession, passion of envy, passion of lust,
Passion of power, passion of sensing,
Passion of the crowd seeing nothing;
And this was Hell.

Then there was peace,
And I walked alone in a little park;
And beyond on the paling primrose of the west
A cool star clung,
One drop of golden rain upon the window glass of
  night.
And as I moved, I saw, like a spider crawling,
A tree of many boughs tangle the star and let it free.
And I thought:
Humanity is a starry tear to Heaven falling,
And like that star,
It seems a moving net of passions tangle it,
But only seems.


## DEMOCAUST

Whose are the hands that are warmed
At the red hearth of war?
And who sit crouched in the smoke
Of the earth where youth is ablaze?

There's a crackle, a snapping,
In the little green valley,
On the lip of the river,

From the green-shuttered belfry;
And amongst the purple sweet clusters
Hid in the leaves of the vineyard,
Jagged fangs are spurting
And maiming the air.
The warm fumes of blood
Exhale from the meadow,
The sleek grasses are red as the embers,
And hot are the flowers with the splashed life of
men.
There's a hiss of escaping breath
From the brands on the hearth that are dying ;
Earth steams with war fire,
And whose hands are warmed?

*Our fingers are chill*
*With the numbness of death;*
*And the coals that would warm them*
*Have yielded their flame*
*Our lads lying wan on the meadow.*

Whose hands are outspread
To the burning of hearts
On the stones of the earth,
Where the star of the young of a people
Has burst into wrath;
And the cinders are smothering
The mouths of the roses,
And the white-breathing lilies;
And choked is the peace of the brook
With grey corpses;
And the soul of the star of the young,
The light of its shining,
Shimmers hot on the wheat –
For a breath –
Then is gone, and the ripe grasses shiver
With the dew of the nightfall of death?
Youth's green limbs are ashes,

Their quick sap is spent.
By whose hands was this kindled?
Whose blood does it warm?

*Our hearthstones are cold.*
*We have fed our young blood*
*To the red fires of war,*
*And the ashes fall dead*
*Our lads that lie white on the meadow.*

## THE WATER-FRONT

On the checker-board
Sky squares and water squares –

Tipsy tugs,
pert stacks,
queening at the dock . . .

On the checker-board
Black sea,
White sky,
kissing corners . . .

Slow steam squirms,
eludes the air. . .

Oh      the salty little clams.
Sniffing!

## THE FIGHT

*Smoke* – more smoke – thickening the air, staining the air blue-grey,
rising on waves of breath, and falling, and filling the channels of
breath, and reddening eyes.

*Smoke* – wreathing the rafters, lying in grey-blue folds over the sloping bank of men – they may be men over there, men's faces and bodies slanting down to the parapet.

*Smoke* – fighting with the glare of the reflectors, fighting the bald splendor of the canvas-padded ring, with the fleshy faces of the seconds, bare bodies, suspender buckles, white shirt-fronts, and the referee's gold watch chain. Smoke – fighting and always losing.

*Smoke* – stung with sudden victories of flame, tiny fireflies that spurt, wink, spread glowing orange over faces framed in writhing twists of blue-grey. Smoke – fighting and losing.

*Voices* – striking down upon the ring, curving like blows around the rocking heads of the fighters, landing on my ears.

*Voices* - glancing over my shoulders, rumbling through my veins. I echo them under my breath: A brave rush, Tony! A fine left, Jack!

*Smoke* – more smoke – I make it myself. My eyes strain through the smother, my eyeballs push and tug at their muscles.

*Bang!* goes the bell. There's the flash of a left, the crook of an elbow, the twist of a nude torso, a right cross darts over a shoulder, into the air above a bullet-head – a locking of arms, the thud of a glove ramming a naked side – a dashing referee cuts the locked forearms, lifts the lowered heads, slices between breasts jamming like savage bulls, and dancing out into the open, leaves a neutral zone behind him – now, as he whirls, before him: *Hiss!* a gloved left lines across the gap, a shoulder blocks the jab and launches a viperous answer into space as a cropped head shifts an inch, the short rights follow in, the lock snaps shut, again the tattoo drumming on the ribs – a muffled buzz of bated breath – and again the referee with his key parts the dovetailed fighters – once more the zone, the hissing leads, frowning looks, tense and bitter, straining for an instant's target – legs spring, feet patter, the lefts leap, the rights zig-zag, miss or glance, locked again – the drumming – sweltering in a fiery space, walled in smoke – *Bang!* goes the bell.

155

*Voices* – Very scientific in his feet: sings a bored Irish voice across the hall – a laugh rolls along the tiers, sweeps into a roar – a murmur of repetitions: What did he say?  Very scientific in his feet – A spatter of belated laughs.

Back to Greece – Two thousands of years ago, several hundreds, some odd months and days, to be exact, and all of Greece that could get there, watched the same thing under the olive-ripening sun on the plains of the Alpheus, at Olympia.  Jack Britton was then Theagenes, a bull of a man, with mountains of muscle flanking the column of his neck – and Ted Lewis was Euthymus, eager, hopeless, and undaunted – then they wore leather thongs upon their hands – and we were Greeks, our backs to the door, and on the further side of the frail boards was black Barbarianism, crushing to break in upon us.

So it was, and is: skill, quivering light brains, muscles flexing and snapping, lefts and rights; and against them, the Brute sagging with sheer gravity of bulk upon the candle-flame of Intelligence.

Greek and Barbarian, skill and Brute, light and dark, over and over – victory and defeat, shuffled confusedly in the smoke.

Something sighs in me when the Brute is baffled, the jeer of the crowd is my jeer – I like the knockout too, but I like it to come as lightning comes, and when it does the triumph makes me sad – for red Brutality outwitted by grey Skill for grey Skill stunned and reddened by dull Brutality.  Which wins?  The Brute, he always winds, and Science never loses.  And Art sits on the sidelines and wins bets from each of them.

Phidias might sign his name under that moving frieze of nakedness, gliding through areas of smoke in ten thousand instants of beauty.

# MAUVE

The rhythm of the sea
Is blent    in undulations of gray satin;
The ashes of burned violets        drift
                        over a sky;
And blurred,
            a magical seed of light
Breaks       in the whorls of a strange flower.
Did you ever see a flower
With core of tarnished silver
                   and five black petals?

*The cover of Robert Alden Sanborn's* Horizons, *1916.*

# FIRST PRINCIPLES

As with all exciting scenes, some come to the table having eaten at many before, and some are taking in their first meals. This final section focuses on the early work of writers before their acclaim. Their different takes on the possibilities of free verse close out this anthology in order to illustrate the fleeting nature of "scenes", and how one person's worldview may only appear as a background reflection in the lives of others.

## Yvor Winters – *The Magpie's Shadow*

*A native of Chicago, Yvor Winters (1900-1968) was known for much of his career as a controversial critic and traditionalist poet who used old forms to explore his own personal themes. This notoriety came after he had spent nearly a decade under the influence of Imagism, publishing several volumes in the 1920's which still have the power to fascinate and inspire. Arriving a bit late to the Imagist party, his first two books, both from 1921, contained many elegant and haunting examples of the genre. For his third book he decided to try something wholly original. Inspired by a line from Rimbaud ("O saisons, ô châteaux!"),* The Magpie's Shadow *is a cycle of 28 aphoristic lines, poems consisting of a mere six syllables in one sentence. Published as a solo booklet by the extremely obscure and short-lived Musterbookhouse in 1922, the set was Winters's most unique contribution to poetic form and remains as beguiling as when it was first published nearly a century ago. Unlike cinquains, however, the form was never adopted by other poets, and the editor hopes that poets looking for new methods might be inspired by these elusive epigrams.*

### I. In Winter

MYSELF
Pale mornings, and I rise.

STILL MORNING
Snow air – my fingers curl.

AWAKENING
New snow, o pine of dawn!

WINTER ECHO
Thin air! My mind is gone.

THE HUNTER
Run! In the magpie's shadow.

NO BEING
I, bent. Thin nights receding.

## II. In Spring

SPRING
I walk out the world's door.

MAY
Oh, evening in my hair!

SPRING RAIN
My doorframe smells of leaves.

SONG
Why should I stop for spring?

## III. In Summer and Autumn

SUNRISE
Pale Bees! – Oh, whither now?

FIELDS
I did not pick a flower.

AT EVENING
Like leaves my feet passed by.

COOL NIGHTS
At night bare feet on flowers!

SLEEP
Like winds my eyelids close.

THE ASPEN'S SONG
The summer holds me here.

THE WALKER
In dream, my feet are still.

BLUE MOUNTAIN
A deer walks that mountain.

GOD OF ROADS
I, peregrine of noon.

SEPTEMBER
Faint gold! O think not here!

A LADY
She's sun on autumn leaves.

ALONE
I saw day's shadow strike.

A DEER
The trees rose in the dawn.

MAN IN DESERT
His feet run as eyes blink.

DESERT
The tented autumn, gone!

THE END
Dawn rose, and desert shrunk.

HIGH VALLEYS
In sleep I filled these lands.

AWAITING SNOW
The well of autumn – dry.

## Babette Deutsch – Selections from *Banners*

> Pin:
> the phoenix
> lays a purple bomb

*An elder stateswoman of American verse for many years, Babette Deutsch (1895-1982) authored seven full collections of poems, two collected versions with additions, four novels and several studies of poetry, including* The Poetry Handbook *which remains in print today. She was also an extraordinary translator, accomplished in translating French, German, ancient Greek, Japanese and especially Russian, which she frequently translated alongside her husband Avrahm Yarmolinsky, head of the Slavic department at the New York Public Library. Throughout her career she wrote in free verse as well as metered verse of various genres, allowing each poem to take the form that fit it best. Her first book,* Banners, *allows for the same cosmopolitan freedom. Her scholarly background contributed to this practice, as she was well-versed in haiku and tanka, forms which she occasionally explored in explicit ways. Her earliest poems show wisdom beyond her years and a philosophy of doing what works before what's fashionable – and that's more than we can expect from any poet working in their early 20's.*

### SEA-PIECE

Dunes overthrown by the wind lie prone to the twilight;
Hold in the foam-darkened hollows and softly moving
Over the pallid sea-marge in slow resurgence
Whispers the ocean.

Threads of foam in the fine sands lingering faintly
Sink as we watch. The touch of the air is colder.
Swift the oncoming clouds. Your lips upon my lips
Salt with the sea-wind.

## SONGS

I would make songs for you:
Of slow suns weighing
Thru pale mist to the river, overlaying
Gold upon silver tissue; or the hush
Of winter twilight when the bushes quiver
Blooming with birds;
Of the easy snow;
Of patient streets, or the theatric glow
Of lamps on crowding faces in the night;
Of sudden gay encounters without words;
Of sorrow quiet in a huddled fight;
Of the release of April winds;
Of death,
That is a stillness without peace, -
Like love, wherefor I am so dumb to you.


## MARBLES

The boys are playing marbles in the street;
Crouched with gay eyes intent on the rough
        ground,
Heedless of storming labyrinthal feet,
Keen only for the lovely sound
Of knocking balls
And colors brightly blent.
Glazed potties, blue and green and lavender,
Gleam near pale stonies' warm eburnean;
Like earth and splintered diamond, agates
        shine;
Glassies are struck alive with sun;
Blood-alleys glow like drops of frozen wine.
Here beauty lies: a bracelet all unstrung
For the March city
While she smiles and stirs
Above the eager gamble, knuckle-down, of

her young jewelers.

Marbles, and March, the tossing wind, and
              the click
Of ball on ball, and wild tumultuous cries,
Anger and laughter, adventure!
A glance and a thumb's short flick:
Rubiesa nd amber and lustrous Carrara to win.
Hope jigs in the heart.
White house-tops sail in the skies.
Romance winks from the dust where the colored
              alleys spin.

The clangorous traffic droans the hurrying crowd's
Nervous relentless tread.
Sunset climbs down the clouds.
Day and the wind are dead.
There are separate ways in the dusk, and lonely
shrill
              farewells.
To lamplit windows and his narrow bed
Each goes, a trifle wistful.
Yet each knows
Prodigious spells
To charm the hours between sun and sun.
The bulging pockets grin; the spoils in reach
Of gloating sight and touch all night must lie.
Each has by heart their palpable sooth speech,
Their singing colors' lullaby.
Marbles, and March, and the dreams of a soft
              Spring night:
Prizes of amber and ivory, lapis and jade.
An arrow of moving light...
They rouse at the joyous noise
Of kissing balls
To the thrill of games unplayed.

## TWO HOKKUS

### ANSWER

You ask for a hokku.
Ask for silence, rather.
It is like trying to ride past the sun.
It is like the words of farewell
Before a final parting.

### SCREEN PATTERN

The hounding wind
Runs shrieking thru the dark.
From a black cloud
The moon gleams like a tiger
Amber-eyed.

## ROMANCE

There are shy woods
Of quickening thin boughs,
Pale jade, alive.

There is a wind,
A tempest and a roar of beaten waters,
Agape with laughing fangs.

There is a darkness,
Tender, terrible.
Gestic, or I remember...?

## HARMONICS

I have come here to be free for an hour or two,
To relinquish to a darkness richly lit,
To the silken movement of infiltering crowds,
The music, the noisy thrill of dischords preluding
        it, -
The morning's fret and the night's restless
argument.
The quarrelling strings and the dim stage are kind,
Rest is in the curtain's velvet fall.
Lovely indifferent strangers put poverty out of the
        mind.
The mutter of traffic is exquisitely drowned
By the low bright liquid swell of belling sound.
I forget...
The milds of mud,
The barren world of mud
And fire; pulling at the boots and biting at the
        flesh.
The watery world
Of sinking corpses.
The filthy dawns,
The flames that crack darkness open and limbs
        apart.
The monstrousness of the unthinkable dead,
The unthinkable living.
The estrangement from known face and places,
The going home to a heap of stones;
The monotonous machinery of hell.
I had forgotten...
The music abruptly stopped,
Chatter arose and applause.  I was aware
Of moving heads, of the close fragrant air,
The flutter of a programme dropped.
I had forgotten the concert-hall
And why I was there.
I passed to the red-lamped exit,

And hearing the newsboys cry
Beckoned.
The pennies jingled; all at once it seemed
Terrible to live.
But curious to die;
And over the music and under the roar or the
        street
The headlines were nothing but print that
        screamed.
There was a sound of war
And of defeat.
I stood there staring at the sunset sky.

## Malcolm Cowley – Selections from *The Little Review* and *Secession*

*Some figures are best remembered for their association with other artists, such as Frances Gregg's friendships with the modernist milieu of her day, and others are remembered as being part of scenes. Malcolm Cowley's fame comes from capturing his scene, and times, in prose and verse. Cowley (1898-1989) earned great praise for his memoir* Exile's Return *(1934), a portrait of Europe and the expatriate scene in the 1920's, as well as his first book of poetry,* Blue Juniata *(1929), which featured gorgeous, haunting prose interludes of life in interwar Europe. The material from* Juniata *included poems written throughout the 1920's, the earliest ones having appeared in* The Little Review, Broom *and* Secession, *a short-lived Viennese journal largely in English. Cowley had a talent for bringing free verse techniques to flash fiction, crafting compelling scenes of people from all walks of life humor and wit. These early poems have aged like fine wine, showing the burst of creative energy and assuredness from this well-loved man of letters.*

### CLINIC

I.

A row of white faces parallels the benches,
which in turn parallel the drug counter and are
at right angles to the aisle which
stops
                    at a given
                                    point.
In another world there are tangents
arcs chords   ellipses
forms more intricate.  But the aisle which
parallels the wall bisects the room and at a
given point
stops.

II.

Mrs. Magrady
grey dress, grey hat, and flesh
dirty grey, undulating
she is dumped on the seat
like an ashcan
                    and what
is the trouble with you today
Mrs. Magrady?

III.

God is an old woman
with dropsy
                or perhaps
you were not created
in his image?

IV.

About the progress of a fly
up these funereal walls there is
a Something
                one remembers
Caesar marching through a burned city
alone.

V.

In a circle of perfume
two girls sit   one with a rose
stuck in a ragged buttonhole and one
with a petalled sore flaunting
on her cheekbone
                    - It ain't my fault
Honest, Doctor.

VI.

If on the windowsill
there were a potted geranium or even
a carnation prettily banal
if a drooping symbolic lily
bloomed in a test-tube

                            anything except
the bloodshot skin of a begonia.

VII.

John Palamos
he comes grinning every day
every day at twelve to show his tumour
three months more   no hope   if only
he would writhe   twist   groan
but his grin
               damnable
                           every line of it
every wrinkle
               on a grey involute brain
acid etched.

VIII.

Against a white skin the brazen
loveliness of a tumour
fistula cancer chancroie
                   It is not
because I have held them beautiful, but rather
that tormented by the chimeras
of youth, by the desire for the white
absolute, by the nostalgia of the immaculate
conception
               I therefore . . . . .

## POEM

One morning during Carnaval they found two swans in the
Public Garden, their long necks twisted, two swans lying
splendidly dead under a magnolia

not yet in blossom and nobody ever knew why they were
killed, whether it was a drunkard, whether an old man tired
of women's bodies and wishing thus to destroy

A more impeccable beauty, or was he young (over
                                      them bends
a domino, black with white moons for buttons, while the
sky like a domino bends more vastly over).

It was a crime of passion; if I have read

of other passionate crimes in curtained alcoves, knife or
poison, they were less splendid than these two dead swans,
O less magnificent than the formal pool, empty without
them, this empty pool which stares

fixedly into a fixed and empty sky.


## FOUR HOROLOGICAL POEMS

I.

If I should go out of this room to walk
down the inevitable street, he says,
the houses would reach out after me
their long tentacular fingers groping
over the sidewalk would clutch and drag me
into the respectability through these yawning doorways
        (Forty a week and a small but growing savings account, a
        cat and two babies, count them two)

172

and yet time is gnawing at the self-assurance of these houses
time is wound
like a worm devouring the entrails of these houses
    O the slow combustion of plaster, O curled yellow
    wallpaper tickling the ceilings
These houses will tumble like rotten fruit to the ground.


II.


And observe if you please the action
Of time upon the pedestrian world,
It runs lightly over the faces and scrawls
its signature in twisted lines under the eyes,
it strips
the flesh from the tendons and causes
the tendons themselves to dissolve into their constituent carbon
and
    nitrogen
it leaves
nothing but a structure of bones       two hundred
bones
    strutting down the street in a business suit
two hundred female bones in crêpe georgette and the empty
    faces dyed with Pompeian, the rouge that beautifies,
and yet those women
wear time as lightly as a feather boa about the neck. . . .
Time is a boa about the neck of all these people
constricting slowly
see they are choking
          their skin
goes dead white
          under the rouge
the bones rattle
          under the skin
two hundred or rather
           two hundred and seven
bones
    parade

173

                    down the street
wrapped
        in a feather
                    BOA.

III.

There is nothing at all that lives in this room by day
and dust sifts down on the soiled coverlet; dust
filters among the lace curtains making queer
amorphous bars across the avenue of escape into the sunset,
tread softly; there are none but the dead remaining here.

But at night something wakens
inthe darkness the clock
ticks viciously at every second
Throbbing its heart out against a tin breast
the minutes stalk
pompously across the field of consciousness
an hour is a time unreckoned
precise and categorical
the seconds hammer on the wall.

At their touch the flesh disintegrates
the mind is reduced to cerebrum and cerebellum
dirty grey whorls like a ball of cotton waste
like a bundle of soiled linen, like clothes cast off and shoddy
the seconds drip from a great heigh
splashing against the tips of my nerves
against the shell of my insubstantial body
and each erodes like geologic rain
a bit of flesh a bit of petrified brain.

          —— I shall countenance this no longer, said the
             Philosopher pick-ing up the clock and hurling
             it out the door, and as he spoke he heard it
             rolling down the circular staircase punctuating
             his remarks very regularly as if it clung to

**174**

rhythm as the sole expression of life, life, I
must have it, Life said the Philosopher
and
returned to his accustomed place
the room was grown so dark he could not see
and the phosphorescence of his lace curtains
dissolved leaving
him out of time and space
whirled in an eddy of eternity

and yet his heart was hammering seventy beats to the
minute
time was throbbing against the fine skin of his
temples
time was dripping through his veins.

IV.

These skeletons which I discuss, said the philosopher,
rise at seven thirty
the rain may fiddle down outside, or the sun turn the
    window shades into vulgar cloth of gold
or the snow fall or any other of the usual phenomena of the
    season but they rise at seven thirty

        O tin alarm clocks detonating simultaneously
in hall bedrooms from the Battery to Yonkers from
coast to coast and agencies in all the principal cities of
the world
O explosive clocks you are very evidently the symbol of
something

AND the quarrel over breakfast at eight fifteen
The hurry of the trip to the subway while the hands of the
    clock of the tower of the building of the Metropolitan
    Life Insurance Company of the greatest city of the
    greatest country – God's country you know it
race past like the Bronx express.

All morning they race over their correspondence

                                        Yours
of the 9th received and in reply we beg to state that
all afternoon boredom seeps out of the pigeonholes of their
desks to pile up in the wastebaskets until
they are seized by a tired jubilation
at five o'clock sharp
    O emotions you also have learned to punch the time
    clock
But if
at any time the alarm clocks failed
simultaneously to function from coast to coast and in the
    agencies in large foreign cities
then perhaps
people would forget the following emotional processes to
wit
    the quarrel over breakfast
    the hurry
    the efficiency the
    boredom and
    the tired jubilation
civilization would crumple like a silk hat that somebody sat
    on and forget to get up
and we should be a frightfully long time straightening out
    the wrinkles.

## Glenway Wescott – *The Bitterns*

*The moniker of "one-hit wonder" is an unenviable one, though in the case of the Wisconsin-born Glenway Wescott (1901-1987) his "hit" is one of the only works by a member of the Chicago literary boom to still be read and admired today. Wescott's novel* The Pilgrim Hawk *was a critical and popular success upon its publication in 1940 and has long outlasted Wescott's other novels, stories and nonfiction. One of the youngest members of the American expatriate community of the 1920's in Europe, Wescott spent much of his travels with the romantic companionship of the publisher Monroe Wheeler, whom he met in Chicago. This travelling life may have inspired his two best-known works,* The Pilgrim Hawk *and* Apartment in Athens, *though little biographical information would help prepare the average reader for his verse. Wescott composed two volumes of poetry early in his career, both in severely limited "private press" editions and to slim recognition. The first,* The Bitterns, *was published by Monroe Wheeler in 1920, when Wescott was only 19. It was limited to 200 copies and featured a patterned paper wrapper by the German expatriate artist Fredrik Nyquist. The extreme rarity of this book, as well its 1925 follow-up volume* Natives of Rock, *has kept Wescott's verse from proper critical appraisal, but the editor considers both volumes, especially* The Bitterns, *to be quite valuable in their own right as haunting codas to the first great era of American modernist verse. The twelve poems in* The Bitterns *exhibit remarkable control of phrase and emotional focus for an author so young, and exude a refined haze of muted grief and possession by the unknown. The editor is pleased to present* The Bitterns *here in its entirety, submitted as an example of a young author who absorbed the energy of his time and made a singular contribution to the literary body of his older peers.*

### I. AFTER-IMAGE

O I have never sought
This image of remembered fear
Which clings to the eye of thought.

**177**

1 have desired rather to create
A balance of beauty as direct
As the hills above the cruel farms,
Or the two eyes of a fawn, —

In ecstasy to separate
Wheat of memory from rust.
But trees by night lift heavy arms,
Or a hawk screams at dawn :

And my sight turns gray as dust.


## II. THE BITTERNS

The bitterns thread the autumn wind,
    Marsh-wind and frost;
The bitterns fly with lidless eyes.
    Sleep is for the lost.

God himself is on the trail
    Twisting autumnal ropes,
The Jew has wandered through the marshes
    And up the lunar slopes.

Hide the inns of sleep from us,
    Drive on the resting leaves.
Autumn gathers the puppets into her
    Wide relentless sleeves.

The waning trees fall steadily down.
    Man with his hurrying breath
Conquers the silver arms of dust,
    Earns the wanderlust of death.

## III. AUTUMN

The gray degraded moon
Sinks in the marshes:
Autumn with her tale of losses.

The loon has left her whimpering mate.

Hung in the sky:
White silent frost, winter.
Hung in the sky; weight
Of the dead moon.

The loon
Has left her mate.


## IV. O GOD, THE NIGHT IS VAIN

O God, the night is vain!
For in the early twilight of pain,
I went out between the stiff trees;
Singing, I gathered hepaticas. Listen, O God,
To the rain and the black litanies.

Singing, I gathered love, I gathered petals
Of twilight. O God, the night is vain!
I hear the night-blooming wings of ravens
Shake in the trample of wind and rain.


## V. THE VALEDICTION OF TWILIGHT

1. *A man speaks.*

"Come closer. I have withered into
A thin dry voice.
I have become a way of speech

Like the cuckoo in the night's border.

"Death will be the last
Caller in the green after sunset,
Will be the last woman
Suave as a poplar, smiling with keen lips.

The sound of twilight complaining
Comes between my voice and other ears."

2. *The comment.*

Hear the end of a man:
He lifts his hands, feels the frost sifting through
    them;
His hands are like grape-leaves, worn thin,
Hesitant where the wind blows two ways.

He could tell where it blows, in the end,
Nods his head, heavy with heedless
Wisdom, into the dusk twisted with trees.

He is a vine, wasted with unwelcome autumn,
Whose roots reach deeper and deeper
Into death.

3. *He speaks.*

"Spring is the fragile season,
Threatened with wind.

Autumn arrives, anyway,
With some sort of fruit,
Scarlet with sweetness, or acid, unlovely,
Autumn comes in its time, and goes.

Spring is the season, precarious,
Heavy with chance.

Be concerned with spring,
With blossoming trees
Like women with pale breasts standing
White in the valley doors,
With frail stars swinging, and petals,
Their ordained descent:
Be concerned with love.

What does the autumn matter,
Age and its bronze fruitage?
I have drunk deep of frost, ether of winter,
I am sleep-heavy and careless."

4.

"Into the valley of woman's love
I walked slowly after the dead,
Their metal feet of echoes.

Valley has followed valley,
Bending the young feet.

Out of the last, that one of memory,
Fruited with images, love and its faint signs,
Death walks slowly before me,
Slowly on the silver feet of echoes."

5.

"She came, the woman I have loved,
Between willow and willow, weeping
For death's unconcern, like rain blurring sand.

What is left of love?—Through the window
I still continue to see willow and willow
And a blood-coloured bird dripping shadow.

But the hepatica-breasts are fallen,
And the gilded leafage of spring is fallen,
Into oblivion.

I am an autumn valley where you walk,
Hearing the wise voices of leaves
Soon to be relinquished."

6. *The comment.*

The splendour of darkness is secret
For old men peering through windows,
With wistful ash-tinted faces,
Who see grackles go darkly down rivers,
And the obscure beauty of moths, knowing
The colour of what is before them.

Living, they look into death
As if through a window of glass.

7. *He speaks again.*

"I am an old man, watching
These windows which wall out obscurity.

Life was a hollow room, from which my eyes
Watched dark omens collecting, even in trees.

Now I am old, and my strength of heart
Is menaced with open ways of wisdom,
Shadows within me grow larger, more splendid,
I am filled with the night which surrounds,
    has surrounded me.

The windows of flesh, a witness, superfluous,
Dissolve like a mist caught between two clouds."

## VI. SONG OF THE CROSS-ROADS

They lie, the implacable peaks,
Folds of water at sunset.
They lie, and toward their glitter,
Red gullies stretch hungry and
Straight as pivots of rain.

I have walked in the straight way,
Implacable over the stones without
Sleep, I know clotted hymns
Of futility, dances of broken feet.

Peace, over there, you parched
Angels of courage, lean,
Haloed with wind. Peace!

## VII. THESE ARE THE SUBTLE RHYTHMS

These are the subtle rhythms, rhythms of sloth:

Mountains which fall in the green swirls
Of twilight as petals, fallen and languid,
Bud in the dawn, and fall again
In the green swirls of twilight, a little
Nearer the stars and the flickering final fires.

These are the rhythms of sloth:
Mountains, my feet on the trails.

## VIII. THIS DREAM WAS MINE

This dream was mine before dreaming:
Snows are exalted on black mountains,

183

Nothing has other meaning.

I cannot hear men coming up
And going down; the hail
Of shadows is and is not.

Fair nakedness of any day
Goes down the inclined wind
Hid in her hair of blackness.

The living flesh goes down
Upon white feet of transience
Into my secret darkness.


## IX. BURIED BENEATH THE WIND

Dimly, buried beneath the wind,
Clink of the sad willows
Gilded with spring.
Victory is immanent,
Night lifts her wide wing.

Clouds rise, shaking their branches,
Showering weary dust,
Rise and go down singing dirges.
Gilded willows ring together,
The helpless season surges,

The sun slides down:
I have not healed
My lame, leprous day;
I am not swift enough to walk
From May to May.

Desert flows beneath my feet,
Drips out of the sky.
But I lie down beside content,

For victory is immanent.
Night opens her deep eye.


## X. THE RETURN

You will return to me,
And dust will be dust again,
Leaves as withered as they will be,
Pain nothing more than pain.

I hear the sob of shadows,
Beside all cripples crawl,
Exalt frost-blighted meadows,
Praise desolation above all;

Carry the imagined cross of Christ,
Am folded in fire's pages.
Bloody atonement has sufficed
For penitential wages.

But you will return to me,
The mesh of death will be shorn,
The mouth that was too hungry
Will laugh its hunger to scorn.

Then I will wear a flesh
Too wild for blood to stain,
Being wild with your new loveliness:
Pain will be futile as pain.


## XI. I, IN MY PITIFUL FLESH

I, in my pitiful flesh
Transfigured, have woven
Music of wilderness.

And now that my old fear is flung
Aside, I will hold
In my hands what hunger has sung
From all the roads where I go
Shame like a red mist vanishes.
On, oh . . .

The desert is shaken with cries:
"Come, and I will be kind."
I am the lover with frightened eyes.


## XII. DESCENT OF SPRING

The choirs of ducks fly northward,
Gold and silver cocks cry spring.

Who can count his bitterness,
Bending the wind to earth,
With a perpetual drip of spring
Over the doors of the adobe houses?

The intangible descent,
Out of the red remote canyons,
Buries the core of rock.

A FINAL POEM...

## CROAK

by Elizabeth Jaeger
from *A Pagan Anthology*

When it darkens and rains
I am not anything human:
I am a frog.
I shelter myself under moss-covered stones,
Blink out at people,
Who passing leave such queer marks,
And say: "Damn the water
          Damn the mud
          Damn everything."
With relish I croak in my nook.

# SOURCES

*Des Imagistes: An Anthology.* London: The Poetry Bookshop, 1914.

*The New Poetry: An Anthology.* Edited by Harriet Monroe and Alice Corbin Henderson. New York: Macmillan, 1918.

*Others: An Anthology of Verse.* New York: Alfred A. Knopf, 1916.

*Others for 1919: An Anthology of Verse.* New York: Alfred A. Knopf, 1919.

*A Pagan Anthology.* New York: Pagan Publishing, 1918.

*A Second Pagan Anthology.* New York: Pagan Publishing, 1919.

*Spectra: A Book of Poetic Experiments.* New York: Mitchell Kennerly, 1916.

*291.* New York (1913-14).

*Broom.* Rome, then Berlin (1921-22).

*The Little Review.* Chicago, then New York (1914-1922).

*Others.* New York (1915-1919).

*Poetry.* Chicago (1912-1922).

*Secession.* Vienna (1922).

**Walter Conrad Arensberg**
*Idols.* New York: Houghton Mifflin, 1916.

**Henry Bellamann**
*A Music Teacher's Note Book.* New York: The New York Poetry Book Shop, 1920.

**Maxwell Bodenheim**

*Minna and Myself.* New York: Pagan Publishing, 1918.

**Witter Bynner**

*The Beloved Stranger.* New York: Alfred A. Knopf, 1919.
*Pins for Wings* (as Emmanuel Morgan). New York: The Sunwise Turn, 1920.

**Stephen Crane**

*The Black Riders and other lines.* Boston: Copeland and Day, 1895.

**Adelaide Crapsey**

*Verse.* Rochester: The Manas Press, 1915.

**Babette Deutsch**

*Banners.* New York: George H. Doran, 1919.

**John Gould Fletcher**

*Goblins and Pagodas.* New York: Houghton Mifflin, 1916.

**Orrick Johns**

*Asphalt.* New York: Alfred A. Knopf, 1917.

**Alfred Kreymborg**

*Mushrooms.* New York: John Marshall, 1916.

**Amy Lowell**

*Men, Women and Ghosts.* New York: Harcourt, Brace and Co., 1917.

**Robert Alden Sandborn**

*Horizons.* Boston: The Four Seas Company, 1916.

**Evelyn Scott**

*Precipitations.* New York: Nicholas L. Brown, 1920.

**Marjorie Allen Seiffert**

*A Woman of Thirty.* New York: Alfred A. Knopf, 1919.

**Royall Snow**

*Igdrasil.* Boston: The Four Seas Company, 1921.

**Mark Turbyfill**

*The Living Frieze.* Chicago: Monroe Wheeler, 1921.

**Glenway Wescott**

*The Bitterns.* Evanston, IL: Monroe Wheeler, 1920.

**Yvor Winters**

*The Magpie's Shadow.* Chicago: Musterbookhouse, 1922.

*All sources in this anthology are in the public domain in the U.S. The assembly of this book would have been impossible without the help of Google Books, the Internet Archive and HathiTrust Digital Library, all invaluable resources in this day and age. The help of the Modernist Journal Project and the Blue Mountain Project, both online repositories of scans of modernist journals, has also been extremely useful. The editor hopes that even more books and periodicals will be digitized and freely distributed, as the altruistic work of these organizations has been of enormous benefit to literary history.*

# RECOMMENDED BOOKS
### by contemporaneous American poets not featured in this anthology

**Loureine Aber**

> *We, the Musk Chasers*. Chicago: Ralph Seymour Fletcher, 1921.

**Geoffrey Faber**

> *Interflow*. New York: Houghton Mifflin, 1915.

**Raymond Holden**

> *Granite and Alabaster*. New York: Macmillan, 1920.

**Oliver Jenkins**

> *Open Shutters*. Chicago: Will Ransom, 1922.

**Robert McAlmon**

> *Explorations*. London: The Egoist, 1920.

**Charles Reznikoff**

> *Poems*. New York: The New York Poetry Book Shop, 1920.

**Lola Ridge**

> *The Ghetto and Other Poems*. New York: B.W. Heubsch, 1918.

**Carl Sandburg**

> *Chicago Poems*. New York: Henry Holt & Co., 1916.

**William Carlos Williams**

> *Sour Grapes*. Boston: The Four Seas Company, 1921.

**Elinor Wylie**

> *Nets to Catch the Wind*. New York: Harcourt, Brace & Co., 1921.

www.ingramcontent.com/pod-product-compliance
Lightning Source LLC
Chambersburg PA
CBHW020854090426
42736CB00008B/374